A Hawaiian Nation I

Man, Gods, And Nature

Michael Kioni Dudley

with an Introduction by
John Dominis Holt

Nā Kāne O Ka Malo Press
Honolulu, Hawai'i

Cover artwork: The communion and intercommunication between man, gods, and nature is depicted in "The *Makahiki* Prayer Dance of a *Kahuna Mo'o Lono*" (a priest of the god, Lono, the god of fertility.)

   Cover drawing by David Kuhia Herring
   Cover design by Belknap Productions
   Publication assistance by Henry Bennett
      Independent Resources, Honolulu

   Published by Nā Kane O Ka Malo Press
   Copyright © 1990 by Michael Kioni Dudley
   Printed in the United States of America

   Inquiries should be addressed to:

   Nā Kane O Ka Malo Press
   92-1365 Hau'one Street
   Kapolei, Hawai'i 96707
   Telephone: (808) 672-8888
   e-mail: drkionidudley@hawaii.rr.com

   The paper used in this publication meets the minimum requirements of American Nation Standard for Information Sciences—Permanence of Paper for Printed Library Materials, ANSI 239.48-1984.

   First printing: 1990
   Second printing: 1990
   Third Printing (Second Edition): 1993
   Fourth Printing: 2000
   Fifth Printing: 2003

Library of Congress Catalog Card Number: 90-184941

ISBN: 1-878751-15-8   paperback
ISBN: 1-878751-16-6   hard cover

For my stepson

Luis Kazuo San Miguel

CONTENTS

Introduction

Man, Gods, and Nature is a particularly welcome addition to the library of Hawaiian literature. Among Hawaiian people, affection for traditional Hawaiian spiritual practices **burns** in the heart with "a hard clear flame." The Hawaiian heart also burns for sovereignty. Both have foundations in the old way of life.

People on islands, who evolve patterns of worship which are both close to nature and mystically linked to powers of the universe, view the human scene and the world around them in quite a different way. Hawaiians, for instance, speak of water in its many forms—rain, mist, clouds, sea, streams, waterfalls, and so forth—as the *wai ola*, "the water of life" or the "living water." *Wai ola* is found at the well-spring of human and natural existence. Its power nourishes all living things and causes them to flourish.

The water of life and man are part of a continuum joined ultimately with all other living things—plants, animals, winds, mountains, and the like. All become inextricably one: united and interdependent and eternally held together by connections that do not break. The chain is made unbreakable by virtue of rules long ago set in the universe—set at the time of Wakea, the Sky Father, and Papa, the Earth Mother—the originators of the Hawaiian people. The laws applied to their times, to subsequent eons down through time, and apply to this very day among those who believe and follow the teachings of *ka po'e kahiko*, the people of old.

For the Hawaiian, the gods who dwell somewhere in space are in fact ancestors of man, *'aumākua,* and collectively are a source of unparalleled power to be drawn upon by the living in effecting the daily tasks of human existence. In Hawaiian religion, thousands of gods exist. Man is the benefactor of both *wai ola* and the *'aumākua.*

In the Hawaiian system, man, the gods, and nature were a three-fold force held together by divine intention in order that all the things of the earth might be protected and nourished. Hawaiians were constantly aware of the binding threads which held together all things great and small. *Pono* as explained by Kioni Dudley is a beautiful process integrating all elements that hold together. *Pono* is the goodness, the well-being, that comes with the balance of existence. The Hawaiian chief did his best to keep his way of life and that of his people in harmony with the powerful forces that made fish swim, birds to fly, clouds to gather above mountain tops, rain to fall, and winds to blow. Forever interconnected, it was the chief's place to give direction to those natural forces and with them to nurture nature.

The mass of material concerning Hawaiian worship is difficult to approach head-on without instruction or help of some kind to take one through the paths laid down for us by the likes of David Malo, Zepheran Kepelino, and Samuel Kamakau. Kioni Dudley has examined the major published sources of the native Hawaiian system and presents a book that captures the essence and the spirit of ancient Hawaiian belief and practice. Dr. Dudley has a gift for presenting profound concepts in a simple manner easily understood. The material is exciting. There is a smooth flow to the book. Every page holds new and fascinating discoveries.

Man, Gods, and Nature is a prelude to *A Call for Hawaiian Sovereignty* and should be read as an introduction to that book. The reader will find both books of *A Hawaiian Nation* an unforgettable experience.

John Dominis Holt

1989

Preface

Come, get to know the Hawaiians—a beautiful people who have a rich cultural heritage and a fascinating intellectual tradition. Hawaiians are people whose lives are closely tied to the islands and to preserving their natural beauty. Hawaiian culture and tradition center around *aloha ʿāina*, love for the land.

Hawaiians today are seeking the restoration of their sovereign nation. What is happening to the islands—the precipitous "development" and unchecked urbanization taking place—is one reason Hawaiians seek to regain control of the land. The paving over of the islands by developers cashing in on the tidal wave of immigration contradicts and opposes everything Hawaiians know in their innermost being to be man's correct relationship with the environment.

The Hawaiians of old developed a philosophical system which explained the universe and its workings, and man's place in it. Like other philosophical traditions, theirs was formulated by observing the way the people actually dealt with the surrounding world. Their philosophy reflected their way of life. And, once formulated, it guided the people in their continuing relationship with the world.

Over the last several decades, few Hawaiians have been taught their philosophical tradition. However, because it so closely mirrored traditional life, even though it is unarticulated and unrecognized, their philosophy still remains an underlying driving force within their culture. As Americanized as they have become, in places where

Hawaiians live and work closely together, they live and act very much in the traditional "Hawaiian way."

Today, if one were to ask Hawaiians protesting "development" to name the cause of the strong feelings which motivate their actions, they might mention the loss of their lands or recount the many injustices they have suffered over the last century. But while many might not mention it, they are also compelled to act on a much deeper level by their traditional world-view which has formed their conviction of what should be the proper, caring relationship between man and nature. That world-view is a basic influence motivating their protest.

Man, Gods, and Nature explains in detail the world-view of the ancient Hawaiians, the thought framework from which they approached the world. Among the ancient chants that have come down to us, there is no one place where this is completely discussed. What is presented here is material collected from ancient chants and stories and from commentaries by the earliest Hawaiian authors, arranged in a way that progressively develops this world view.

Generations have passed since the death of the last Hawaiian who lived and functioned only through the ancient thought-context. Much has been lost. One should see this book as a modern-day reconstruction, put together under less-than-ideal circumstances. The world-view developed is consistent with the actions of Hawaiians described in early writings. It explains their thoughts and actions. Yet this book is not intended to be the last word—it stands only at the threshold of needed research.

Further, it must be made clear that Hawaiian tradition is rich with variants. Travel by canoe between the islands was not an everyday occurrence, and the relative isolation encouraged alternative ways of explaining things. This book does not try to present or comment upon all of the variants. It develops a single thread of traditional thought, selecting material consistent with what the author sees as the thought-background from which the ancient Hawaiians approached the world. The author also does not contend that **all** Hawaiians were aware of **all** of the philosophical aspects presented here. But he does maintain that all the topics discussed here were the essential, fundamental components which over the centuries came to form the prevailing thought-background from which Hawaiians approached the world.

Getting into contact with the Hawaiian world-view is essential for anyone interested in Hawaiian culture. Only when one is aware of this traditional thought context, and only when one can think from within this framework, can one fully understand the traditional literature. Many of the mistranslations and misunderstandings which have plagued Hawaiian writings for the last two centuries stem from authors not having taken into account the traditional thought-framework from which Hawaiians experienced the world.

Man, Gods, and Nature aspires to give the sovereignty movement roots, to ground it in the Hawaiian philosophical tradition. The book is also written for non-Hawaiians. As readers understand how Hawaiians function and interrelate with the land, sea, and sky, it is hoped that they will also see how it is essential for the Hawaiians' survival that they have lands—inalienable lands on which they can live their culture and propagate their race. It should also be seen that much of Hawaiian philosophy is not only eminently suitable for island living, but that it has value for non-Hawaiians when applied in modern life today.

A word needs to be said about the use of the words, "conscious," "sentient," and "cognitive." Although philosophers over the centuries have carefully defined each of these terms, clearly distinguishing them from one another, no such distinction is made in this book. The words are used interchangeably to indicate that nature can "know" what is going on and that it can "act on its information." In Hawaiian thought, nature goes about things in a thinking way, much as man does.

"Spirit," "soul," and "mind" are also frequently used interchangeably, and they should be taken as indicating the same entity unless otherwise stated.

Acknowledgments

Much of what is written here is a non-technical rewriting of parts of the author's doctoral dissertation, *A Philosophical Analysis of Pre-European-Contact Hawaiian Thought.* I would like to acknowledge my doctoral committee members at the University of Hawai'i: Roger T. Ames, chairman; Eliot Deutsch, K.N. Upadhyaya, and Graham Parkes, all from the Philosophy Department; and Rubellite Kawena Johnson—the Hawaiian specialist on the committee—from the Indo-Pacific Languages Department. I also want to thank Professor J. Baird Callicott, of the University of California, Santa Barbara—a pioneer in the area of environmental ethics—for his support and suggestions for the dissertation.

Professor Stephen Boggs, Ph.D., for many years deeply involved in the Hawaiian scene, has been very generous with his time, reading the text and making suggestions.

Henry Bennett, of Independent Resources, has been very helpful both with editorial assistance and in guiding the book through publication.

The artwork on the cover is by David Kuhia Herring, a student at Leeward Community College. All the drawings David produced as we worked out *"Makahiki* Prayer Dance of a *Kahuna Mo'o Lono"* were striking.

Buzz Belknap and his staff at Belknap Productions are pleasant, generous, and talented — such a pleasure to work with in creating the cover designs for the books.

I want to salute the young men of the Nanakuli Hawaiian boys' club, *Na Alaka'i Mua* (The Leaders of Tomorrow). Their enthusiasm for their Hawaiianness and their willingness to **work** on projects to preserve their cultural heritage has been a continuing inspiration to me. Much of the drive I have had to finish these books has been powered by the desire to help bring about a Hawaiian nation for them.

Many people of Nānākuli have worked with me in efforts to get the public school system to educate Hawaiian children as Hawaiians. Deeply involving themselves in activities these books so roundly support, they too have been a continuing source of encouragement.

I also want to pay tribute to my parents, Willard and Melva Dudley, for the high priority they placed on education for their children, and for their unfailing belief in my visions and dreams during the years of pursuing my doctoral degree and working on these books.

I want to recognize my aunt, Marie Mac Donald, for her enthusiastic support over the years. I am grateful too to my mother-in-law, Yoshiko Kamioka, for her generous encouragement of this project.

Daniel Kenji San Miguel, my stepson, did the drawings found in the text of this book. Patiently working with me through the many revisions required to give form to what I could not visualize and could describe only vaguely, his original drawings have captured my intent and expressed it with fascinating creativity.

The person who stands out as having given the most in support of all my endavors is my wife Doris (Kolika) Sadako Dudley. I am grateful for her love and for the many sacrifices she has made over the twelve years of study, research, and writing that I have given to these books. My greatest treasure, my best friend, and my most willing helper, these books would never have been completed without her.

If one is to think as a Hawaiian, he must leave his own thought framework and move into another. When there is no one to show the way into the other, one is at a loss and may stumble about for years, meeting only with contradictions. I did. My stepson, Luis Kazuo San Miguel, was responsible for many of my early insights into the Hawaiian thought context. *Man, Gods, and Nature* is dedicated to him.

Michael Kioni Dudley, Ph.D.

Honolulu, Hawai'i
Makahiki, 1989

A Fish Story

IF ONE MEETS a Hawaiian fisherman loading his nets and gear into his truck, he never asks if the man is going fishing. He might ask if the man is going *holoholo*, "out for a ride," or he might ask if he is going to the mountains. But if he asks if the man is going fishing, the man will take his gear back out of the truck, and that will be the end of the fishing for the day. For the fish will "hear" and know that the fisherman is coming, and they won't be there when he gets to the sea.

A common reaction to hearing something such as this is to dismiss it as a "fish story," as something told to fascinate children, or as a tale about the "exotic natives" fabricated for tourists. "No one is expected to really believe it," one might think as he gets on with the important, **real** things in life.

One also hears that old Hawaiians are sometimes observed talking to plants and trees before picking their flowers—asking before taking—and that they often leave offerings when they take something of significance.

"There is value in carrying on cultural traditions, but this perhaps is carrying thoughtfulness and sensitivity to nature to an extreme," one might think.

Many Hawaiians also believe that they have ancestral spirits (*'aumākua*) who dwell in animal or other nature forms. Among these are the *mo'o* (lizards), various birds and fish, rainbows, various cloud forms, forests, and mountains. The best known of the ancestral spirits, perhaps, is Pele, the goddess who dwells in *Kīlauea* volcano. Pele, in her lava form, flows down among the people on occasion. Hawaiians know the nature forms to which their families are related. And they think of their ancestral spirits, and the nature forms they inhabit, as family members. When they encounter their *'aumākua*, they recognize the occurrence as special: a greeting, or possibly a warning, or an affirmation of the correctness of some action.

Hearing of such practices, a non-Hawaiian might perhaps question whether people really do such things today. And if Hawaiians actually do—and if they really put stock in what they are doing—he might judge them as foolish.

Foolish: that is the bottom line in the modern Western assessment. People of today must earn a living in an economic world where bottom lines are what counts. One rises or falls on how well one understands business and on how well one can work within the economic structure. The world today runs according to the Western man's perspective. That perspective treats nature as a commodity, as scientifically measurable forces, and as resources to be used, rather than as fellow beings in an interrelating world community. What doesn't correspond with Western man's world-view is seen as of little value and as something that can, and probably should be, ignored.

Such an attitude is not new in Hawai'i. Early traders and missionaries who arrived in the islands thought in the same way. As they taught Hawaiians to read and write, they also taught them to think as "modern Westerners" and to repudiate their culture and their traditional world view. This negative attitude toward Hawaiian thought and customs has prevailed among most of the people who have come to the islands over the years. Today many modern

Hawaiians feel embarrassed or uncomfortable when cultural practices such as those related earlier are discussed.

But an approach to life developed over thousands of years must contain much wisdom. During the two millenia that Hawaiian people lived in these islands, they developed a complete and unique system of thought. This explained their world and how things in it interrelated with one another, and also how man fitted into the complete picture. Like the Indians, Chinese, Japanese, American Indians, and others, Hawaiians approached the world from a distinctively non-Western perspective. This Hawaiian perspective or world-view formed the basis for a philosophical tradition which, though very different from the modern Western view, does explain the world just as adequately. One can function in today's world while approaching it from the traditional Hawaiian thought framework just as well as one can by approaching it from the Western thought framework. Certainly, for island dwellers, there must be special insights and wisdom in the Hawaiian approach.

To understand Hawaiian thought, one must first realize that the Hawaiian truly experiences the world differently. One who believes that the fish hear, who asks plants for permission before picking their flowers, and who thinks he is related as family to many of the species of nature surrounding him, obviously experiences and reacts to the world differently from one who does not. In the Hawaiian view the world is alive, conscious, and able to be communicated with, and it has to be dealt with that way. Man participates in a community with all of the species of nature, a community in which all beings have rights and responsibilities to one another.

To understand the Hawaiian, one must move into his thought framework and see nature from his perspective. This requires venturing into a perspective entirely different from the Western view, and living at least for awhile from that new perspective.

This book tries to lead the reader along the way. The Hawaiian world-view is built, adding—piece by piece—the background information that fills out the completed picture. The book begins by discussing how knowledge was passed on in ancient Hawai'i. A view of how Hawaiians thought the universe was structured is then presented, followed by how they conceived of matter and spirit, and how they viewed both as "cognizant" or able to act in a knowing and causing manner. Following this Hawaiian evolutionary theory is studied.

Only then can these ideas be assembled to discuss what the Hawaiian meant by nature being alive, conscious, able to be communicated with, and related to him as family. A chapter relates this perspective to modern scientific theory. And finally, through stories and examples, the reader will observe how the Hawaiian approached the environment as a participant in a sentient community, and how he lived his *aloha ʻaina* (love for the land.)

Passing On Knowledge In Ancient Hawai'i

LEARNING WAS HONORED in ancient Hawai'i. Those intellectually gifted were constantly challenged to higher and higher levels of competence and knowledge. Although outstanding thinkers came from every level of society, formal education was not generally available to commoners. To acquire a sufficiently broad basis of knowledge to make meaningful advances, one had to be trained as a chiefly child in the court, or as a candidate for the priesthood, or as a *haku mele* (a chant master).

Since Hawaiians did not have a written language, knowledge was passed down through stories and proverbs, through riddles, and through formal chants.

Haku mele learned the great traditional chants, recited them for the people of their time, and passed them on to the next generation. *Haku mele* also composed chants. They were the scholars: they studied and reflected upon the content of their repertoire, discussed it, and critiqued it with their peers. At times they would propose changes to incorporate the insights, discoveries, or events of their generation into an ancient chant.

The most knowledgeable and most respected among the *haku mele* were the *kākā 'ōlelo*. In *Kepelino's Traditions of Hawaii*, he says of them:

5

The *kakā 'olelo*, who might be one person or a group of
people, judged the nature of this and that ancient oral
tradition. They corrected things according to their
decisions, and occasionally discarded things of this or
that tradition which were not correct. These people
chanted as their occupation. And they became a family,
a family of *kakā 'olelo*.[1]

It was to the assembled *kakā 'olelo* that the *haku mele* (chant
masters) must come if they wished broad acceptance of
newly composed chants or if they had proposals for changes
in traditional chants. The meetings are described as taking
place in a special house, the *hale nio*.

When the bards had composed their *mele* [chants], they
met at the *ni-o*, a house where were assembled also the
critics, the wise men, literati, and philosophers, who were
themselves poets *haku mele*; and the compositions were
then recited in the hearing of this learned assembly,
criticized, corrected and amended, and the authoritative
form settled.[2]

One pictures the *hale nio* as a "school" where new ideas
were presented, where they were argued and defended
against tradition in lively discussions, and where grave
decisions were made on what versions would be passed on
to future generations.

One must be "economical" in oral transmission. The
material that could be passed on was limited by the *haku
mele* able and willing to memorize, and later teach, a share of
it. Chants passed on for centuries were relatively few. A
popular chant telling of a chief's great feat or a love chant
composed about a favorite chiefess might survive one or
two generations, but as events and individuals receded into
history, the popularity of chants concerning them similarly
waned.

While various types of chant were used for passing on bodies of knowledge, the safest vehicle for transmission was the name chant of an *ali'i nui*, a high chief. A name chant included the genealogy of an *ali'i* (chief). It was through the recitation of his name chant that one proved his hereditary right to rule. As long as a chiefly line endured, it was certain that its genealogical name chant would also be passed down.

The economy of chant also demanded that all information passed on for centuries would tend towards its most concise form. Chants would be cut by expunging expendable thoughts and contracting what remained, possibly through rephrasing it in multiple-meaning language.

Since words with multiple meanings are frequently used in the great chants, many passages have several layers of meanings. The short "Maui chant" in the *Kumulipo*, for instance, is a collection of almost all of the stories told in Hawai'i about that famous demigod. Through use of words with multiple meanings, carefully worded passages tell, or make reference to, three, four, or five stories at one time. One knowledgeable about Maui's feats can find references to more than thirty different stories in the scant sixty-five lines of the chant.

If a chant was in danger of being lost it might be attached to another more popular chant, or its most important thoughts might be incorporated into another chant as a perpetuation technique. The great genealogical name chants of the *ali'i*, such as the *Kuali'i*[3] and the *Kumulipo*, are composed of several ancient chants grafted on to the original genealogical name-listings so that they would not be lost.

The *Kumulipo* is a famous genealogical chant for the line of *ali'i* that comes down to the Kamehameha and Kalākaua dynasties. In tracing the ancestry of the chiefs back to their earliest origins, it presents an evolutionary theory which is one of the most important intellectual accomplishments of the ancient Hawaiians. Evolution is central to their understanding of man's place in the world and of his relationship to the things of the world: evolution explains how man is kin to the world of nature. The *Kumulipo* is the source for much that will follow in these pages.

The Hawaiian View Of The Universe

IN STUDYING THE TRADITIONAL Hawaiian view of man and the environment, it is helpful to understand how the ancient Hawaiian thought the universe was structured.

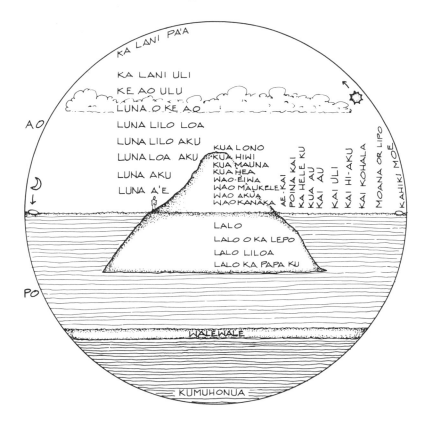

Figure 1. —THE WORLD OF THE HAWAIIAN — ILLUSTRATING DETAILS GIVEN BY DAVID MALO in *Hawaiian Antiquities* (Honolulu: Bishop Museum Press) 1951, pp. 12, 15, 16-7, 25-6. Drawing by Daniel Kenji San Miguel.

As shown in Figure 1, the Hawaiian structured his view of the world as a series of belts or levels reaching out from himself and his island. He named levels in the sky above, and within the earth beneath. He named levels of progress up the mountainside and belts around the island as one moved out to sea.

Hawaiians conceived of the firmament as an overturned bowl. The early Hawaiian writer David Malo named nine levels of the sky above man's head, reaching higher and higher into the dome of heaven. The sun, moon, and stars moved across the dome at the highest level, *ka lani pa'a*.[1] When the sun set, it sank into the sea and continued its circular motion beneath the earth, rising again in the east on the next morning.

Hawaiians had names for the belts of the sea surrounding an island. They named at least eight stages before reaching the farthest and deepest belt which they called *moana*, the deep ocean. They also called the deep ocean *lepo*, which ordinarily means "underground," or *lewa* which generally refers to "areas of the air and sky." The deep sea had still a fourth name: *lipo*, which means "deep blue black."[2] (Shallow water appears green, but its color becomes progressively darker and darker blue as one reaches deeper and deeper water.)

There were also names for various strata of the earth beneath the surface. Malo recorded four. Hawaiians had observed that the base of the islands descended down into the sea. But while they thought that a seabed underlay the entire ocean, it was a common view that the islands floated in the sea, unattached to the seabed.[3] The concept of floating islands can be seen in the story of the demigod

Maui and his brothers when they attempted to tow Kaua'i over to O'ahu and attach it to Ka'ena Point. Maui hooked Kaua'i with the great fish hook, Mānai-a-ka-lani. His brothers, having been commanded not to look back, paddled the canoe for O'ahu, while Maui chanted a charm. They towed the island all the way to Ka'ena Point. But as one of the brothers got out of the canoe, he could not resist looking back to see if the island was really there. That broke the spell. The line holding the island broke, and Kaua'i floated back to where it is today.

The seabed deep beneath the floating islands was covered with a layer of slimy silt (*walewale*)[4] in which coral and other living things grew. There is a story that Kapu-he'e-ua-nui fished up a piece of coral. He was about to toss it away when a *kahuna* (priest) told him to offer a prayer. He did, and it turned into the island of Hawai'i. He fished up another piece, and prayed; then another, and another, until he had fished up all of the Hawaiian Islands.[5] All over Polynesia a somewhat similar story is told concerning Maui. He is said to have fished up, not coral, but the islands themselves with his sacred bait. Among the islands he is credited with fishing up are the north island of New Zealand (which is called Te Ika A Maui, "The Fish of Maui"), Rakahanga, the Tonga group, and Hawai'i.[6]

The whole of the underworld seems to have been referred to as *pō*. *Pō* was said to be "a vast sea out of which land was born."[7]

Sometimes the word *pō* is used more specifically to designate a certain area of the underworld. For instance, *pō* is the place in the underworld to which souls descended to dwell after death. According to one source, a soul passed through the lowest of the four levels of earth in order to reach this $p\bar{o}$.[8]

$P\bar{o}$ is a word with many meanings, and it is not always easy to nail down which is intended. It is perhaps used vaguely out of necessity, since the areas within $p\bar{o}$ are not clearly distinguished and their geographical locations are not clearly defined. But to compound the problem, "$p\bar{o}$" has many other non-spatial connotations. It can mean the past, the dark or black, the dimly seen, the unknown, that which is ancient and only dimly known, night, the spiritual, the mystical, the void, nothingness. $P\bar{o}$ also has to do with origins. It is that original state or being or time or place from which all things come. And in a later period, $p\bar{o}$ is the time of dwelling in the original homeland and/or is the homeland itself. The islands settled along the way are also called $p\bar{o}$ or *tumu* $p\bar{o}$. (Most Polynesians use T where Hawaiians use K. Thus *Tumu* $p\bar{o}$ is the Polynesian spelling for what is written in Hawaiian as *Kumu* $p\bar{o}$.)

Chants and Drawings Detailing Cosmic Structure May Also Be Maps

It is very common in Polynesian thought to find discussion of how the world is structured tied to discussion of how all things began. This is not surprising because cosmic structure and cosmic origins go together naturally. And the economizing of chant demands that famous works which will be passed on for centuries will have many levels of meaning. For this same reason, one might expect that chants and stories of cosmic origins will have, woven in with them, accounts of other, later kinds of "beginnings" and developments. And they usually do, if one looks for them. One finds among creation stories the mention of the

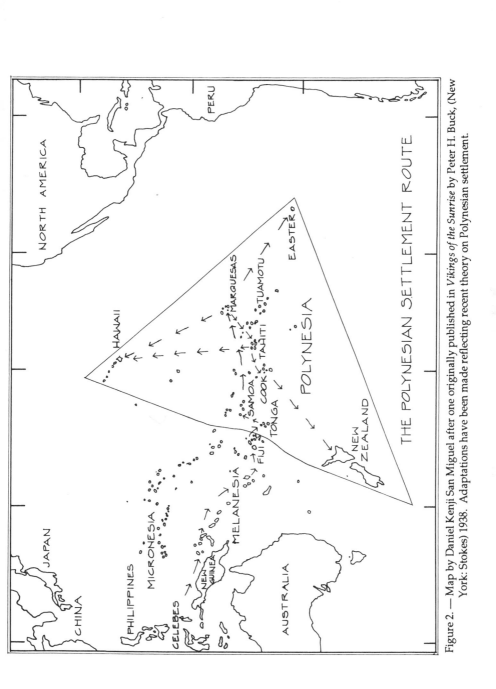

Figure 2. — Map by Daniel Kenji San Miguel after one originally published in *Vikings of the Sunrise* by Peter H. Buck, (New York: Stokes) 1938. Adaptations have been made reflecting recent theory on Polynesian settlement.

original homelands from which the people came. In creation chants one also might find details about early travels and islands settled in Polynesia on the way to the present island home.

Drawings of how the world is structured are available from several island groups. One must examine these with care as well. A drawing that at first sight is taken to depict how the universe is structured might, upon more careful study, be seen to be primarily a map of where the people came from and how the world was viewed by their navigators.

Interpreting chants and drawings in this way has not to my knowledge been done before, and what follows should be looked upon as speculation rather than as established fact. For many years, I found the cosmic views depicted in diagrams from the Tuamotu Islands and from Mangaia in the Cook Islands puzzling, not only because they were too simplistic, but because they seemed to contradict celestial information that must have been known by the great ancestral navigators who settled the islands.

The ancient-styled, long distance voyaging canoe, the *Hōkūle'a*, sailed to Tahiti and back in 1976 and again in 1980 without using any modern instruments, even a compass. Instead it used only ancient knowledge and navigational techniques. Between 1985 and 1987 the *Hōkūle'a* sailed from Hawai'i to Tahiti to Rorotonga in the Cook Islands and then to New Zealand, and returned through Tonga, Sāmoa, Rarotonga and Tahiti to Hawai'i, a distance of half way around the world. Its Hawaiian navigator, Nainoa Thompson, again guided the entire journey using only the ancient art of sailing by the stars, winds, waves, and other natural phenomena, with no compass or other modern instruments. With this great journey the *Hōkūle'a* demonstrated that the Polynesians had the knowledge and the capability to navigate the great discovery and settlement expeditions around the Pacific, and to sail from island group to island group just to visit.

I had trained with the *Hōkūle'a* crew for that journey, and was convinced that Polynesians of the past had left their navigational knowledge with their descendants. But where?

It appeared that the knowledge must be in their drawings and creation chants. They just needed to be viewed from a different perspective. To look for clues to interpret the vestiges of their knowledge, one needed to immerse oneself in what must have been the navigators' thoughts and views. I did that. What follows is the fruit of that endeavor.

In Mangaia in the Cook Islands the world of man is pictured as perched on the top of a great coconut. Above the top of the coconut are ten levels of sky—a parallel to the levels of sky named by the Hawaiian. The sun and the moon, interestingly, move in their circular pattern on the first level, closest to man. They rise through a hole in the top of the coconut in the East and set through a hole in the coconut in the West. The interior of the coconut is called 'Avaiki, a transliteration of Hawai'i.

There are names for the various levels of the interior of the coconut as one descends to the root. The highest level of the interior of the coconut is the realm given to the first man, Vatea. After Vatea found a wife-mate, they both climbed through the opening used by the sun and moon, and humans have since lived on top of the coconut. The first man, and the various levels of the interior of the coconut, are

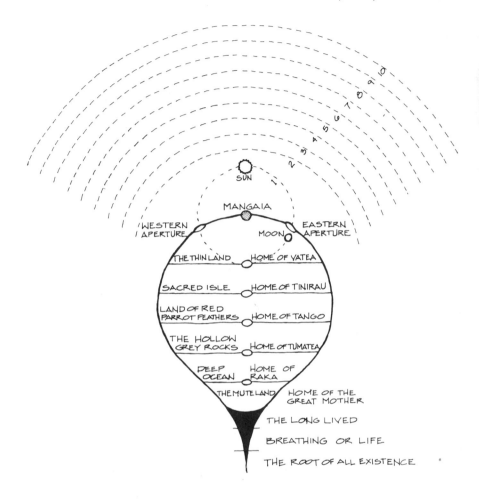

Figure 3. — VIEW OF THE UNIVERSE —IN MANGAIA, COOK ISLANDS.
Artwork by Daniel Kenji San Miguel after drawing in *Myths and Songs from South
Pacific* by William Wyatt Gill (New York: Arno) 1977, p. 2.

the children of the Great Parent who lives at the very bottom
of the inside of the coconut. Beneath the great Parent is a
taproot called *Te-aka-ia-Roe*, the Root of All Existence.[9] This
drawing (Figure 3) is mesmerizing in its similarities to the
Hawaiian world construct—with its numerous levels of sky
and levels within the earth. There is even a tradition of a
"taproot" at the bottom of the cosmos in Hawaiian thought.

I did not see the drawing as a map, at first. This was natural. Because of the way Western minds have been trained to look at drawings, Westerners instinctively see Figure 3 as representing a cross section of the earth and nothing more. It must be recognized, however, that Polynesian art of that period was simple, two dimensional, one-flat-plane work. Stories and references depicted in their drawings often occurred on different planes. But, like the European artists in the first millenium, the Polynesians did not separate into different pictures things happening on different planes. This Mangaian drawing shows places which would better have been depicted on the surface of the coconut mixed in with the places and beings thought to exist inside the coconut. While it would have been desirable to create both a surface map and a cross-section of the interior, either because of the state of their artistic ability, or because someone could always be depended on to be there to explain the distinctions, they combined the planes together in one flat drawing. It is now our task to recognize this, and to separate out the different planes.

With this in mind, let us look again at the Mangaian situation. The first man and the first woman came to Mangaia from Ra'iatea in the Society Islands. In those days Ra'iatea was called Havai'i or, as the Mangaians spell it, 'Avaiki. It lies to the east of Mangaia, in the direction of the rising sun. The story of Vatea coming from the first level of 'Avaiki below, and of his climbing through the opening used by the sun, is telling us of the arrival of the first people from Havai'i, the most recent (or first level back) of the islands they formerly inhabited. This interpretation seems to be confirmed by the statement of Potai, a wise man of Mangaia, who commented on the arrival of Captain Cook:

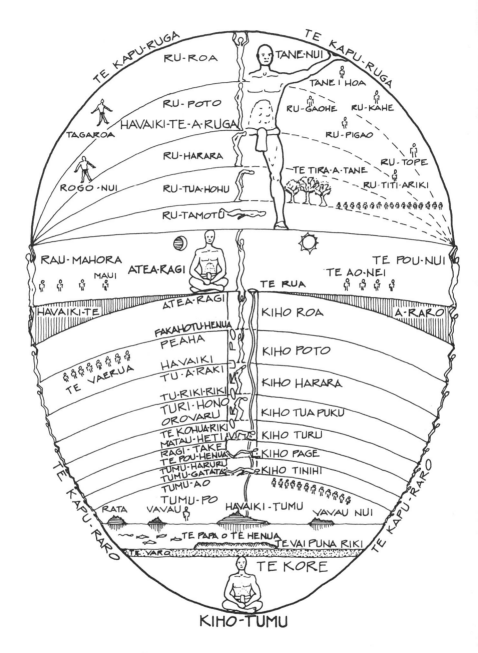

Figure 4. — VIEW OF THE UNIVERSE — ANAA, TUAMOTU ARCHIPELAGO
Artwork by Daniel Kenji San Miguel after a drawing in *Tuamotuan Religion*, by J.
Frank Stimson, Bernice Pauahi Bishop Museum Bulletin 103 (Honolulu: Bishop
Museum) 1933, p. 63.

"Surely, friends, he has climbed up from the-thin-land (the highest level of 'Avaiki), the home of Vatea."[10]

The concept of man climbing up from levels of land beneath is common also to drawings found in the Tuamotu Archipelago. A diagram presented by Stimson shows men climbing up the **sides** of the cosmos to the world of a presently inhabited Tuamotu island.[11] (See Figure 4.)

If this climbing is seen as man's journeying, and one traces back down to where he has come from, what one finds is worth the trip. For one reaches *Tumu Pō*, or "The Source of *Pō*," which is clearly a place, and is like another world. In the drawing, *Tumu Pō* has a sea in which lie islands, seemingly of Tahiti, and possibly of Tonga. These are the islands from which the Tuamotuans came in ancient times.

It seems then that these Polynesian people referred to the earlier-settled islands from which they had come as the "The Source of *Pō*" (*Tumu Pō* or *Kumu o ka pō*), and that they conceived of this as lying beneath them. They portray man as coming from those islands to the presently inhabited islands by coming up the sides of the world. Figures of climbing men tie the seas and skies of the two areas together. The diagram, then, is a navigational chart telling that Tahiti and other islands are beneath the horizon, and telling that the people once journeyed from those islands to the presently settled Tuamotu island.

Why did the Tuamotuans picture the lands from which they came as lying directly beneath them and inside of the world? Because they only made flat, single-plane drawings, and what they required in order to adequately depict what they intended would have been either a surface map or two

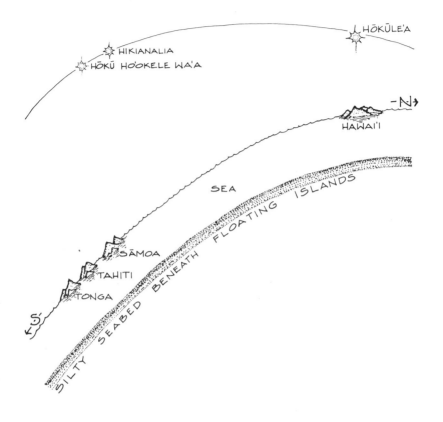

Figure 5. — POLYNESIAN ISLANDS — SINGLE PLANE DRAWING LOOKING
WEST. Drawing by Daniel Kenji San Miguel.

cross sectional drawings—a north-facing cross-section, and a
west-facing cross-section.

To clarify what is meant, consider the relationship of
Hawai'i to the rest of Polynesia. The ancestral homes of the
Hawaiians lie over the horizon and "beneath" Hawai'i. One
can picture the relationship of these islands in a single-plane
view looking West.

But as one takes that same scene and pictures it along a
single plane looking north, the southern islands pull over

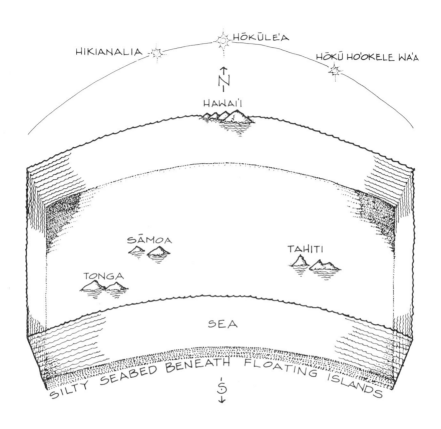

Figure 6. — POLYNESIAN ISLANDS — LOOKING NORTH. Drawing by Daniel Kenji San Miguel.

and situate themselves "underneath" Hawai'i. This is the way they appear on flat maps of the Pacific today.

Looking at modern maps we do not think of Tahiti, Sāmoa and Tonga as being "inside of" the world. Why is it that when we look at the Tuamotuan map we see these islands as under the Tuamotus and "inside of" the earth? The reason is that the Polynesian map mixes a navigator's map with one of interior cosmic structure, and we view it as interior structure alone. The two must be separated.

How the Hawaiians Pictured the Cosmos

We do not have an early drawing of the cosmic structure from Hawai'i. Figure 1 at the beginning of this chapter is a mock-up from details given in the works of David Malo. It is quite possible that the Hawaiians did not picture the cosmos in the same way the Mangaians and the Tuamotuans did. Those islands were settled long after the Hawaiians had broken off from the Polynesian settlement movement, and the Mangaian and Tuamotuan diagrams could follow a later developed tradition. Perhaps it is unwise to latch on to their cosmic diagrams too quickly.

Consider how early Polynesian settlers of Hawai'i might have viewed the world. They had come from a continent into an island area off South-East Asia. Their predecessors had thought of the world as flat. As they moved into new territory, progressing down the Melanesian chain, every time they reached one island, they could already see the next. They had no reason to reassess their view. It was only when they reached out toward Fiji, Tonga, and Sāmoa that they had to begin developing a new understanding of the cosmos, how it lay and how it worked. Their exploring expeditions began using stars in order to successfully navigate long distances.

They now experienced new things about the world, and their perception of the world had to change to coincide with their experience. As they sailed farther and farther, they found other islands which lay under the paths of the stars to the north. They had no idea how big the Pacific was, but they did know that islands disappeared from sight behind them. As they sailed into the prevailing easterly winds, they thought of themselves as climbing. As they sailed downwind into the south-west, they thought of themselves as descending. They possibly came to picture their world not as round, but rather as inclined. At some time they also came to see it as bowed, probably because as they approached an island they could see its mountain tops come into view first, and then slowly see the rest of the island emerge above the horizon.

Because of our round-world view, we have difficulty seeing the world as anything but a complete circle, and we project primitive peoples as picturing themselves sitting on the top. The early Hawaiian might rather have viewed the world as like the crescent between the 9 o'clock and 12 o'clock segments of a circle. And he may have pictured his island, not at the top, but as lying in the 11 o'clock area, while the 12 o'clock area lay further upward into the wind.

That this was the ancient Hawaiian and Polynesian view seems to have support in statements found in early Hawaiian writings. David Malo, for instance, notes that when the prevailing north-east trade winds blow, the whole northern quarter of the heavens is spoken of as "up," and the southern quarter, towards which the winds blow, is spoken of as "down."[12]

Writing about the arrival of the first Hawaiian people, he states,

> It has been said, however, that this race of people came from the *lewa*, the firmament, the atmosphere; from the windward or back of the island (*kua o ka moku*). The meaning of these expressions is that they came from a foreign land: that is the *lewa* or "region of air." [13]

Every Polynesian island had a front, the side facing away from the wind, and a back, the side turned into the wind. And it is true that coming from the Marquesas or Tahiti, as the two Hawaiian settlement groups did, they had to sail up into the wind far enough to get parallel with the islands, and then would ride the trade winds "down" into the back of the islands. As Malo states correctly then, this people came from the *lewa* (the area upwind) and landed at the back of the islands.[14]

Carrying the discussion of "upwind" further, interestingly the Sāmoans call the white man a *pa-lagi*, a "sky buster." Today this is interpreted as meaning that the white man came from the heavens with the gift of the Christian religion. But when the first Westerners arrived, it probably meant that he had "come from upwind," from the heavens.

In the Tuamotuan drawing (Figure 4), one can also see that man, having reached the Tuamotus, nevertheless continued to climb up into various levels of the heavens. I view this as their depiction of man continuing to travel to other upwind islands such as the Marquesas Islands.

Let us go to the seashore and try to see further into this matter. East is generally upwind in the northern tropics, and upwind is "higher," so let us sit on the eastern shore. Look into the distance up at the horizon. If we see a great sailing canoe take off now and head for the horizon, where will it go when it gets there?

At the horizon, the sky touches the sea. While the canoe will continue sailing on the water, when it reaches the first level of sky, it will sail through it. If we picture the sky as touching the sea in the way that a rainbow touches the earth, we can feature the canoe remaining on the sea but sailing through the several bands of the rainbow. As the canoe climbs higher and higher into the wind, and higher and higher on the face of the earth, it sails through higher and higher levels of sky where they touch down to the earth.

The Tuamotuans and others who depict men and islands in the sky are really trying to convey that people dwell upwind, higher on the earth than they.

The writings of William Ellis on the Hawaiian view further confirm what has been developed here. Writing of Kamapua'a and his visit to Tahiti, he states,

> He travelled from Oahu to countries beyond the heavens, namely, beyond the visible horizon, the boundary where they supposed the heavens to be joined to the sea.[15]

The world from the Hawaiian perspective, then, is perhaps more correctly depicted in the following diagram.

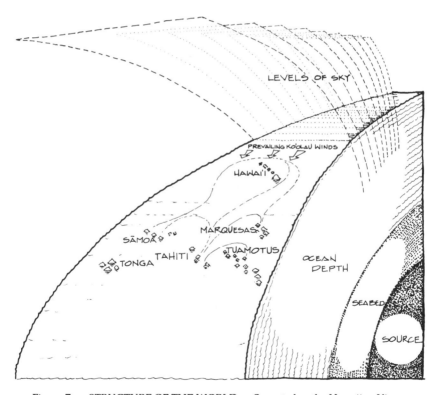

Figure 7. — STRUCTURE OF THE WORLD — Sugested as the Hawaiian View. Drawing by Daniel Kenji San Miguel.

P̄o As the Ancestral Home

Where is *p̄o* according to the ancient Hawaiian view? *P̄o,* or *Tumu P̄o,* is that land from which the early ancestors of the Polynesian people came and to which the souls of the dead are thought to return. Since the time of Fornander, who wrote in the mid-1800s, scholars have pointed out ties between the word "Java" and the word "Hava-iki" or "Hawai'i" as it is found in variant forms found throughout Polynesia. Sava-i'i, the name of the biggest island in Sāmoa; Hava-i'i, the ancient name for Ra'iatea (an island in the Society Islands); and our Hawa-i'i, all mean something like "Little Java" or "Offspring of Java." The Maoris of New Zealand refer to their ancient homeland as Hawa-iki. The Mangaian people use the variant form, 'Ava-iki. According to Fornander, "All islanders say their ancestors or gods came from the West."[16] And there seems little doubt that the original homeland of the Polynesians was either Java or some related island in that general area.

In the Tongan Islands, the first Polynesian island group to be settled, there is a common awareness that the souls of the dead follow the rays of the setting sun to the west to find the ancient homeland where they join their ancestors. Sāmoa, which was settled next, has a tradition that all the souls of those islands make their way to a *fā-fā,* or "leaping place" at the western point of their western-most island, Savai'i. There they leap into a tidal pool at the sea and make their way to their ancient homeland, following a western course within the sea. Rarotonga has a similar leaping place on its west shore. The western-most tips of both Lāna'i and O'ahu in Hawai'i are called Ka'ena Point, and are the *leina,* or "leaping places" from which souls of those islands make their departure for their eternal homeland.

Hawaiians spoke of reaching *pō* by following the rays of the setting sun to the West and descending to it along with the sun. So it is likely that the original native Hawaiian view of where *pō* lay was that it was downwind, in the direction of the setting sun, far below the horizon. Once the period of the great inter-archipelago voyaging had passed, great variation developed among traditional stories and ideas as they were passed on over the centuries in the far separated areas of Hawai'i. As traditions gathered around remnants of facts from the voyaging period which could no longer be understood, some bards came to teach a *pō* that was within the earth, below the islands. It seems that the original concept was so ingrained in the chants and in the thought patterns of the haku mele (masters of chant) that, even though they might have forgotten that "beneath" meant "over the horizon, downwind, in the direction of the setting sun," they could not bring themselves to clearly define where it was, "beneath them." And so they left its whereabouts as vague, speaking of *pō* as lalo (beneath, below, or downwind) and *lepo* (south or dirt).[17]

Bottommost Source in the Cosmic Structure

In considering again the cosmic structure, it appears that the Hawaiian saw his world as inclined somewhat up into the wind. There were several belts of sky above, and the sun and moon passed through the highest level. All of the islands—Hawai'i and the known Polynesian islands to the south, and the original homeland in the far southwest — were thought to be islands floating at the surface of one great ocean. Underlying the whole expanse of the ocean was one continuous slimy, silt-covered seabed from which coral and islands came forth. But what lay beneath that seabed?

Two diagrams from the Tuamotus published by Stimson
show an originative source beneath the silt-covered seabed
in the place called *Tumu Pō*.[18] According to his charts, the
source is divine. In Mangaia in the Cook Islands, where the
universe is pictured as a great coconut, "The Great Parent"
lives at the very bottom of the inside of the coconut. And
beneath "The Great Parent" is a taproot called
Te-aka-ia-Roe, the Root of All Existence, which constantly
sustains, and "insures the permanence and well-being, of all
the rest of the universe."[19]

The idea that the cosmos grew up from some bottommost
source is common to much of Polynesia. In a number of
islands, this source is a root. The first people to reach the
Hawaiian islands probably brought that idea with them
also, for growing up from some bottommost point seems to
be one of the patterns upon which evolutionary thought in
ancient Hawai'i is formed.

Several Hawaiian traditions hold that the god
Kumu-honua (which means "Earth Source") dwells at the
bottommost point of the cosmos.[20] In one genealogy,
Kumu-honua (Earth Source) is mated with Lalo-honua
(which means "Earth Bottom" or "Earth Depth").[21] In
another genealogy he is mated with Ka-ma'i-'eli, "The
Vagina in the Depths."[22] And according to Malo, at the
beginning of creation Kumu-honua was the father of
Ka-mole-o-ka-honua, "The Taproot of the Earth."[23] This
Kumu-honua who is spoken of as active in these most
primal stages of cosmic generation is, in some traditions,
said to be a manifestation of the god, Kāne. No matter who
Kumu-honua is, his presence in these stories demonstrates
that the Hawaiians, like other Polynesians, viewed the
bottommost source as active, conscious, and causative.

The prologue to the *Kumulipo* chant also makes reference to the structure of the world. It speaks of the *ka walewale ho'okumu honua ia* "the slime at the bottom of the sea which gives forth the land," and it mentions *ke kumu o ka pō*, the source of *pō*, which seems to be *Tumu Pō*. It seems also to designate the original progenitor of all as *pō*, in its pristine state, active and causative, existing at the beginning, alone. This *pō* might be seen as the bottommost originative source of the universe.

Spirit And Matter In Hawaiian Thought

FROM EARLIEST TIMES man has had encounters with "things" he could not see and over which he had no control. Whatever they were—natural phenomena, human fantasies, or actual spirits—he thought of them as "spirits." Some cultures have viewed these beings as forming a different realm from matter. Spirits might assume somewhat material forms that could be seen, such as ghostly forms, but they did not need to have any material form at all.

Ancient Hawaiians made a clear distinction between spirit and matter. Spirits were such things as gods, ghosts, souls of men, and the spiritual essences within material things. Matter was everything else: things that were hard and heavy and which could be felt and lifted; things that had body. *Aka* and *akua* are both words for "spirit." They are used in contrast with "matter" as it is defined in this paragraph.[1] *Aka* and *akua* are sometimes used interchangeably, because their meanings overlap. But they also have quite specific individual meanings.

The Usage of *Aka* in Hawaiian Thought

Aka is frequently translated as "essence," as well as "spirit." In Hawaiian thought "essence" is the spiritual quality of a thing, or the spirit within a thing. When offerings were made to the gods, the gods ate the "essences" of offerings put out for them. A prayer offered at a graduation, for instance, encouraged the gods to eat the *kino aka*, the spirit form, of the animal brains. "Look upon your disciple, and take up to yourselves the essence of the graduation and of the graduation meat." *E ike i ka 'oukou pulapula, e lawe a'e 'oukou i ke kino aka o ka ailolo a o ka 'i'o.*[2]

Another prayer said when making a food offering to the gods was "Yours is the essence, O god, ours the material part. *'O ke aka ka 'oukou, e ke akua, 'o ka 'i'o ka mākou.*"[3] When the gods had finished and departed, there was no difference that could be observed in the offerings. Food or other material forms were seen to remain the same. Yet the essences or spirits in the offerings were thought to be gone. Gods, being non-material spirits, were thought to eat the *aka*, the non-material essences.

The Usage of *Akua* in Hawaiian Thought

In the dominant current of Western thought there is a fundamental separation between humanity and divinity. God, who is eternal, infinite, all-powerful, and all-knowing, is said to have created the finite world, not out of himself, but out of nothing. All of creation, including man, is "other than God." For man to equate himself with God, or to think of himself as part of God, is considered blasphemy and traditionally is thought to be a heinous sin.

In many other cultures, however, such differences between human and divine do not exist. Some peoples have no concept of a "Supreme Being" or "Creator God" who is by nature "other than" his creation. They do, however, claim to experience a spirit world in which beings more powerful than they are concerned for them and can be called upon for help. These "gods" or "divine beings" are often thought to be souls of the deceased who either are earlier direct ancestors of the individuals they help, or are leaders or "holy men" honored by the whole people. Examples of these kinds of "divinities" are the saints of Roman Catholicism and the Buddhas and *bodhisattva*s of Buddhism.

The Hawaiian words *akua* and *'aumakua* are often translated as "god" because they designate the kind of beings in a spirit world who assist man in his needs. But in the specifically Hawaiian development of the Polynesian terms, they are closer to the concept of the Catholic "saint" or the Buddhist *"bodhisattva"* than they are to the Christian concept of "God."

But *akua* does not always have even as exalted a meaning as "saint" or "ancestral helping spirit." When the Hawaiian used *"akua,"* more often in his own mind he intended to convey the simple concept of "spirit" or "spirit consciousness." Only in certain applications of the word did he mean "divinity" or "helping ancestral spirits." And when he did, he intended to speak of nothing other than basic spirit being/s who were invested with extraordinary additional spiritual power (*mana*).

Akua Means "Sentient Spirit" or "Spirit Consciousness" or "Cognizant Entity"

An *akua* is a "sentient spirit," a "spirit consciousness," or a "cognizant entity." By this I mean that an *akua* is a spirit-entity which knows and wills, has capabilities for desires and emotions, and also has capabilities for the extra-sensory powers of telepathy, clairvoyance, precognition, and psychokinesis. Once one begins to project "spirit consciousness" with this full meaning onto the word *akua*, and ceases to think of it as meaning "god" or "divinity" or "saint," many problems of misinterpretation fall away.

An example can be seen in the following story. While it was common for Hawaiians to attribute spirit consciousness to things, what they intended was evidently misinterpreted by Lorrin Andrews, the author of the *Dictionary of the Hawaiian Language* printed in 1865. Andrews states that *akua* was "the name of any supernatural being, the object of fear and worship; a god," and he adds, as explanation, that when the Europeans first arrived, Hawaiians applied *akua* "to artificial objects, the nature or properties of which Hawaiians did not understand, as the movement of a watch, a compass, the self-striking clock, &c."[4] Closer scrutiny of his examples shows that all three of the things to which the Hawaiians applied the term *akua* were things which moved from within, and seemingly of their own volition. To Hawaiians, they exhibited consciousness within. When Hawaiians spoke of *akua* in relation to watches, self-striking clocks, or compasses, they were misinterpreted as taking entire objects for gods when in fact they were commenting about the knowing and causative spirit-entity they thought must be within.

There is also a troublesome passage in *Kepelino's Traditions of Hawaii* which is cleared up by a correct understanding of *akua*. The problem occurs in Kepelino's discussion of different kinds of spirits. He contrasts angel spirits with the spirit-souls of men. According to Beckwith's translation, Kepelino calls man a god. She writes, "A spirit that belongs to a body is a spirit combined with a body and called a man, a god, meaning one who dies." *"Uhane pili kino, he uhane ia i huipuia me ke kino: a ua kapaia he kanaka, he 'kua, he mea make ke ano."*[5] Neither the sentence itself nor the context in which it is stated offers any reason, however, for Kepelino to be calling man "a god." In this passage he is talking about spirits that are joined with matter, such as in the soul-body composite that forms man. Kepelino intends to say that man is composed of "a human form (*kanaka*) and a spirit consciousness (*akua*)," nothing more. This interpretation fits the context. And it uses *akua* in a manner consistent with the interpretation of this book. A more correct translation would be, "Some spirits cling to bodies. An example is a soul combined with a human body. In this case you have a human form and a spirit-consciousness (*akua*), a body and soul (*akua*). Unlike angels, this kind of being dies."

Akua, then, basically means "spirit consciousness," "cognizant entity" or "sentient spirit." *Akua* may refer to any kind of spirit: a spirit thought to animate a clock, a spirit living in a some form of nature, the soul of man, or an ancestral spirit ("a god").

A Spirit Adapts to the Form It Indwells

An *akua* can dwell as a pure spirit. Or it might dwell within matter. When it does indwell matter, it is distinguished from the matter it inhabits. *Akua* are non-material beings who can enter and leave material things: the spirits dwelling within humans during life enter at conception and leave at death.[6] A possessing spirit (*akua*)[7] can come upon a person and later leave.

When a spirit indwells a form, it adapts itself to the functions of that being. It assumes the limitations on its abilities to know which are proper for the physical form it inhabits, while retaining, in potency, its capabilities to know in other ways. The *mana'o* or "mind" of man, for instance, is an indwelling spirit (*akua*) which takes on the advantages and limitations of human form. Although it can experience broadly through the senses, its extra-sensory perception is curtailed while in the human body. A person who can use his extra-sensory powers is said to do so because he has more *mana* (spiritual power) than others.[8] Greater *mana* enables his *akua* to act beyond the ordinary limits of his physical form. Once the spirit leaves a body again at death, it is free of bodily constraints on its ability to know. It is thought to have knowledge of the future and of things in other places, to have some control over matter, and to have a much more comprehensive view of events and situations.[9]

Consciousness in Matter

In the mainstream of Western thought, spirit and matter are clearly distinguished. God, angels, and the souls of humans are said to be spirits. Spirits are able to think and to will. In man it is the spirit or soul alone that thinks and wills. All things other than God, angels, and souls fall within the realm of matter. Matter is incapable of thinking, willing, or of any other type of knowing. This cut and dried distinction made by Western thinkers causes major problems. One arises in explaining how the thinking soul in man can tell the body, which is material and cannot think, what to do. For a thing to understand a communication, it must be able to think. If the body is incapable of thinking, it should not be capable of understanding orders from the thinking soul.

Hawaiians do not run into this problem because they do not use spirit to explain all thinking and willing in beings. They view matter as also being capable of thinking and willing.

They see man's material body as itself being conscious and as using its own thinking and willing powers.[10] This can be seen in the *Kalanimanuia* story where various parts of the body are depicted as conscious, self-identifying, and able to do as they wish. In the story, Kalanimanuia is killed, but his spirit is later restored to life. Initially the spirit assumes the form of a rat, but this is "worshiped" (*ho'omana 'ia*) and eventually develops into a human form. This body is not whole, however, and Kalanimanuia lacks the manly beauty necessary to win the woman he desires. One night, hearing a racket in the house, Kalanimanuia calls out "Who is that?" and receives the reply: "I am Puakuakua, the soles of the feet of Kalanimanuia." "I am Moi, the knees." "I am Lohelua, the two thighs." "I am Limuhuna, the hair." "I am Mohoea, the eyes." The text goes on to say, " At this, the beauty and fine appearance of Kalanimanuia returned to him."[11]

The idea that the parts of the material body are conscious and act on their own is further also seen in the way Hawaiians refer to actions they have done. "The feet walked," "The ear heard," and "The hands picked," are common phrases, and reflect a view that various parts of the body are responsible for their own activities.[12]

Clearly, then, in Hawaiian thought things may be created of spirit and matter, but both spirit and matter are capable of thinking and willing. It is thus that they interact and work together.

Evolutionary Theory In Polynesia

THE MOST COMPREHENSIVE of the endeavors of the *Kumulipo* is its development of a theory of evolution of species. Evolution was not a new concept to the Hawaiians, but rather one which they further developed. The basic theory is also found in New Zealand[1] and, in less clearly worked-out form, in Tahiti and Sāmoa.[2] Its presence in Sāmoa, one of the first-settled ancestral homelands of the Hawaiians, argues convincingly for its presence in Polynesian thought from a very early period.[3]

Examining some evolutionary theories developed in other Polynesian islands will allow us later to more clearly distinguish the indigenous Hawaiian development by contrasting it with what preceded it. The following material comes from Sāmoa:[4]

> Another myth told by Turner attributed the earth, rocks, trees, and everything to the marriage of fire and water. Then the cuttle-fish fought with the fire, and the fire conquered; the fire fought with the rocks and the rocks conquered; the large stones fought with the small stones, and the latter conquered; the small stones fought with the grass, and the grass conquered; the grass fought with the trees, and the trees conquered; the trees fought with the creepers, and the creepers conquered; the creepers rotted, swarmed with maggots, and the maggots grew to be men.[5]

This story does not speak of one species evolving from another, other than man from the creepers. But it does demonstrate a survival of the fittest, or triumph of the fittest, as the species spread to new realms and modes of habitation.   Grass grows over the stones and moves on, covering the land.   The trees grow up and out of the grass. Creeping vines climb up the trees and choke out their sun, killing them.   This spreading and conquering which accompanied the evolutionary advance of species was catalogued, at least from the battle of the grass with the small stones, in a sequence consistent with present day thought.[6] Darwinism argues that species advance blindly, and it teaches that those survive which—as the result of "chance" mutations—are the most adaptable to changes in the environment.   By contrast, as the Sāmoan material above demonstrates, Polynesians believed that all of the species of nature are conscious, that they are aware of problems militating against their advance, and, that in devising successful war strategies, and in fighting and winning battles, they are responsible for their own evolutionary advance.

A chant from the Maori people of New Zealand shows great sophistication in evolutionary thought. It traces things of the presently seen world back to "nothingness" or "pre-material-being," and then explores that pre-material state. The Maori mind seems to have revelled in abstraction and to have searched its realms deeply. They emphasized the evolutionary period of the pre-concrete, pre-material world.

The following Maori evolutionary chant was given to Richard Taylor:

The First Period:

From the conception the increase,
From the increase the swelling,
From the swelling the thought,
From the thought the remembrance,
From the remembrance, the consciousness, the desire.

The Second Period:

The word became fruitful;
It dwelt with the feeble glimmering;
It brought forth night [*po*]:
The great night, the long night,
The lowest night, the loftiest night,
The thick night to be felt,
The night to be touched, the night unseen.
The night following on,
The night ending in death.

The Third Period:

From the nothing the begetting,
From the nothing the increase,
From the nothing the abundance,
The power of increasing, the living breath;
It dwelt in empty space,
It produced the atmosphere which is above us.

The Fourth Period:

The atmosphere which floats above the earth,
The great firmament above us, the spread-out space
  dwelt with the early dawn,
The moon sprang forth;
The atmosphere above dwelt with the glowing sky.
Forthwith was produced the sun;
They were thrown up above as the chief eyes of heaven;
The heavens became light,
The early dawn, the early day,
The midday. The blaze of day from the sky.[7]

Study of this chant shows that at the beginning of the First Period of pre-material-being, "thought" is conceived and comes forth.

After thought or thinking exists there can be recall of past thoughts: "remembrance" can exist. The combination of the two capabilities, thought and memory, is "consciousness." Then can come "desire." According to Maori thought, then, from the first stages of evolution, nature is thinking and conscious. In the second period of pre-material-being, the "word" produces $p\bar{o}$ (night or darkness or nothing) and $p\bar{o}$ ends in death. In the third period, which is finally a period of material-being, from the nothing (pre-material-being) is born the living breath (the life-force), and it produces the atmosphere above from which the rest of the material world evolves.

Hawaiian Theory of Evolutionary Origins

While Maori evolutionary investigation specialized in an abstract tracing back through pre-material-being and beyond to an ultimate beginning, Hawaiians applied themselves to speculation on the emergence of life forms in the cosmos. They devised an evolutionary theory that encompassed the various forms of life they encountered in their world of experience. They had no microscopes, so they began with the smallest living being they could see, the coral polyp. They lived on an island chain in the middle of the Pacific which had relatively few plants and animals in comparison with the continents. Their evolutionary ladder for animals went from birds to reptiles, then to pigs, dogs, and rats, and then to men, with no other animals in between. The only land mammals they encountered in their island world were rats, dogs, pigs, and men.

They were careful catalogers, and their developmental sequence corresponds well with modern theory. Rubellite Kawena Johnson writes:

> The order of species in the Kumulipo is from invertebrates in Chant One to vertebrates in Chant Two. The order of progression is a sequence of forms growing more complex in the scale of evolution from coelenterates (coral polyp, coral), to annelids, nematodes (worms, segmented and unsegmented), echinoderms (asteroids, holothurians, echinoids), and mollusks (sea snails, mussels, i.e. pelycypods; shells, gastropods). Some arthropods are classified with mollusks, indicating contrasting exceptions.

She concludes:

> From all appearances, however, the Hawaiian invertebrate phyla and their appearance in the ascending scale of evolutionary complexity correspond rather well to taxonomic norms for invertebrate groupings.[8]

The *Kumulipo* in its entirety is an attempt to present a cohesive and systematically thought-out interpretation of the underlying organizational structure of the cosmos and the beings in it. That the evolutionary theory it presents so well parallels evolutionary theory taught today is a tribute to the careful study of Hawaiian thinkers.

Ultimate Source or Cause in the *Kumulipo*

In chapter three, the prologue of the *Kumulipo* was interpreted as passing on information about the structure of the cosmos. It was noted then that there are several levels of meaning in the prologue. Here we consider the prologue as telling of the originative "being" from which all creation evolves.

Hawaiians observed the theme of birth throughout nature. All plant and animal life was born. It was logically consistent, then, that the universe was similarly born. Tracing evolutionary development back to more primitive forms, the Hawaiian finally arrived at the coral polyp. According to the *Kumulipo* chant, the coral polyp was born from Kumulipo and Po'ele, which are often said to be generative principles, rather than beings. And Kumulipo, Source-of-the-deepest-blue-black-ocean (*lipo*), and Pō'ele, Black-pō, were born from *pō*.

Let us examine Rubellite Kawena Johnson's translation of the *Kumulipo* before tracing further.

> When space turned round, the earth heated
> When space turned over, the sky reversed
> When the sun appeared standing in shadows
> To cause light to make bright the moon,
> When the Pleides are small eyes in the night
>
> From the source in the slime was the earth formed
> From the source in the dark was the darkness formed
> From the source in the night was the night formed
> From the depths of darkness, darkness so deep
> Darkness of day, darkness of night
> Of night [Pō] alone.
>
> Did night [Pō] give birth
> Born was Kumulipo in the night, a male
> Born was Po'ele in the night, a female
> Born the coral polyp
> Born of him a coral colony emerged.[9]

The first lines speak of the earth and the sky, leaving the impression that the coral was thought to be descended from them. More careful scrutiny, however, reveals that heaven and earth are mentioned only as a means of designating the time for the emergence of the coral. The chant reads:

"**When** the earth heated, **When** space turned over... Did [$P\bar{o}$] give birth.... Born was Kumulipo, a male; Born was $P\bar{o}'ele$, a female.... Born the coral polyp...." The coral seems, then, to have come forth directly from $p\bar{o}$,[10] as did the heaven and the earth. Tracing origins to their ultimate source, one seems to find as the source of all things "$P\bar{o}$ existing alone" ($P\bar{o}$ *wale n\bar{o}*).

If $p\bar{o}$ existing alone is the ultimate source, however, is $p\bar{o}$ a place, as was said earlier in interpreting a different level of the prologue's meaning? Or is it the realm of the unknown? Or, as suits this interpretation, is it a "being" or a "force"? And if it is a being or a force, is it composed of "pure matter"? Or is it "matter imbued with spirit"? The composers of the *Kumulipo* have left no answer to these questions.

From the Beginning—
A Conscious Material Universe

But it is not essential to establish whether the cosmos at the beginning was thought of as "pure matter" or whether it was thought of as "matter embued with spirit." More important is that the "material universe" from the beginning was thought of as conscious and self-acting, and that its evolutionary development came from within. David Malo writes, "In the genealogy called *Kumu-lipo*, it is said that the land grew up of itself, not that it was begotten, nor that it was made by hand.[11]

From the very first lines, the *Kumulipo* teaches cosmic self-action. Using Beckwith's translation, the chant begins:

At the time when **the earth became hot**
At the time when **the heavens turned about.**[12]

There is no outside agent causing this change. It comes
from within. Movement from within demands a conscious
decision and a causative act of will. If the heavens and the
earth had continued to lie in eternal quiescence, there would
be no need for either decision or causation. However, a
change from eternal stillness to movement requires both.
And since the word used in the Hawaiian is *kāhuli* rather
than *huli*, this change to movement is clearly described as
taking place from within. Hawaiians, then, clearly ascribe to
the material universe a decisive action, and the
consciousness this implies.

Earth and heaven were thought to accomplish their
desires just as did man and the rest of nature. In another
familiar story, the earth (mother) was thought to grow warm
with passion for the sky (father), longing for its embrace and
sexual union. The rain that is so common near the
mountains at night was said to be the tears of the sky father
weeping for the embrace of the earth mother. It was
through the relationship of the sky and the earth that all
things were nourished and became fruitful. Every night the
Hawaiians observed the Milky Way in the heavens as it
turned over when it reached its zenith in the sky (Any kind
of bowed thing moving overhead looks, from underneath, as
if it turns over as it moves across the zenith). Every night
they also observed that the Milky Way touched the earth in
two different places (Because of its relationship to the earth,
the Milky Way seems to move around the sky. It touches the
earth at two **different** points on the compass each night of
the year. Moving completely around the sky during the
year, in some months it runs north-south across the heavens,
in other months it runs east-west). Hawaiians thought of the
Milky Way as the semen of heaven which fertilized the earth

where it touched the horizon. Its strange nightly movement in the sky argued convincingly for its activity. For the Hawaiian, the material universe was indeed alive and conscious.

Sentient Spirits Enter Evolving Forms of Nature

In discussing the early evolution of the material world, the *Kumulipo* makes no mention of *akua* or spirit. *Akua* has a prominent place in the evolutionary process, but the word does not appear until after *pō*, heaven and earth, *Kumulipo* and *Pō'ele*, the coral polyp, the starfish, sea urchins, crabs, clams, and other shelled animals of the sea have already arrived on the evolutionary scene. Thereafter, however, akua is repeatedly mentioned in the first four *wā* or chapters of the chant. These chapters trace evolution up through all the plants and animals except the dog, pig, and rat. They contain a repeated refrain used to introduce most pairs of species in the evolutionary advance. It is called the "Refrain of Generation":

> Born is the [species named] living in the sea.
> Born is the [species paired with it] living in the upland.
> The male member slides in with exultant jubilation.
> The female enjoys. Coming together sates the sexual
> hunger of foliate life.
> Knowing, causative, **spirit-being** (*akua*) enters, having
> no human characteristics.
> Born is the male quality, as the narrow, precipitous
> stream.
> Born is the female quality as the broad, receiving lake.
> (This author's translation)[13]

This "Refrain of Generation" is repeated forty-four times as species after species is introduced in the *Kumulipo*. It must be considered one of its most important statements. It affirms the fundamental principle that nature evolves through sexual reproduction.[14] But more importantly, it tells of the indwelling of evolving nature by spirit consciousness: "Knowing, causative spirit-being (*akua*) enters having no human characteristics." "*O ke akua ke komo, 'a'oe komo kanaka.*"

Further, the repetition again and again of the statement that *akua* enters suggests that at each evolutionary step additional spirit consciousnesses are added beyond those already possessed by the parent species. If this is true, the many species of the plant and animal kingdoms, including man, should be seen as indwelt by a number of spirit consciousnesses (*akua*). Indeed, such a view was found among the early Hawaiians. The *Kamapua'a* chant, for instance, reflects a view of man in which he is composed of body and a number of spirits which form his spirit nature.[15]

Hawaiians, then, saw themselves as reflecting nature, and viewed all of nature, including the cosmos itself, as reflecting them. If man could think and act, then the material universe should do likewise. The Hawaiians' world was filled with conscious beings which formed an interrelating community with them. They depended upon, cared for, and communicated with the surrounding world of nature, and it depended on, provided for, protected, and communicated with them.

The Nature of the *Akua* Which Enter Nature

What was the *akua* like which is described as entering matter in the early stages of plant and animal evolution? Where did it come from? Could the *akua* that entered the species have been an almighty, all-present, infinite, and eternal "Supreme Being" whose existence preceded all material being? There is no evidence for a belief in any kind of "Supreme Being" in Hawai'i prior to the white man's arrival. To say that the *akua* which entered nature at the earliest stages was thought to be anything like the traditional Western concept of God reads too much into the word.

In the New Zealand Maori chant quoted earlier in this chapter, in the realm of pre-material-being, the first thing to be conceived and to come forth was thought, then remembrance. These composed the consciousness, which then experienced desire. In attempting to define what the Hawaiian meant in the "Refrain of Generation" of the *Kumulipo* when he spoke of the *akua* which entered into the evolving species, the Maori chants offer an important hint. At every level, the entering *akua* was spirit consciousness: knowing, causative, non-material being. The Hawaiian consistently gave *akua* this meaning.

In the Hawaiian context, did this spirit consciousness pre-exist matter? Or did it co-exist with it from the beginning?[16] The question of what the *Kumulipo* taught as existing at the very beginning is not clearly determinable at this late date. The *Kumulipo* speaks only of conscious matter existing and evolving at the very beginning, and its first mention of *akua*—as the spirit being which enters the natural forms as they evolve—comes only after the cosmos and thirty-four species of animal and plant life have already evolved. If one is to use the *Kumulipo* as a guide, then, it can only be said that *akua* coexisted with conscious matter by the time *akua* began to enter the animal and plant forms of nature.

The Hawaiian Experience of Reality

The *Kumulipo* traces evolutionary development through higher and higher species until it finally reaches man. After the *Kumulipo* reaches man, it traces the genealogy of the chiefs from the first man down to Lono-i-ka-makahiki, a chief reigning on the island of Hawai'i in the 17th century. The chants of the Hawaiians told them that they had descended from the cosmos itself and from its many plant and animal species. They were related as family to all of the forms of nature from which they had descended. They felt a kinship with nature which is not experienced by people who see a break between mankind and the species of nature which have preceded them in the evolutionary advance.[17] In the Western world, where the cleavage is most pronounced, animals are disdained as having senses but no reason; the plant world is recognized as alive, but in no way even aware; and the elements of the cosmos are treated as inert objects which follow mechanical laws. Hawaiians, on the other hand, view all of these beings as sentient ancestral forms which interrelate with them as family.

The difference in how the Hawaiian and the Westerner experience reality can be illustrated by the reaction of a person in an unfamiliar building who, rushing to a meeting late, opens one door and finds a storage room filled with canned items, then opens another which is the front door to a lecture in session. Entering the "empty" storeroom elicits a totally different response than entering lecture room full of people, even though he might not know a single person in the disturbed lecture. Canned items on shelves mean nothing to him; they lack that which gives them significance: consciousness. The storeroom is "empty." The people in the lecture give meaning to the other encounter. It is their consciousness, their seeing him blunder which makes the difference. The surprise and embarrassment the person experiences come about because of the people's consciousness, and with it their ability to relate and to help or hurt. These are all perceived immediately and undifferentiated from the appearance of their bodies in his total comprehension of the scene. Recognized consciousness makes demands on the perceiver, demands for correct behavior and correct relationship. For the Hawaiian, there are no empty storerooms. Confronting the world about him, he experiences conscious beings at every turn, and along with this their interpersonal demands.

Further, there is also a real difference between coming upon someone recognized as a relative and meeting someone who is not. In perceiving one who is kin, a person experiences not only an added awareness of relationship, but also an emotional feeling of belongingness.

As the Hawaiian views the world, what he actually **sees** is the same as what the Westerner sees, but what he **perceives as seen** is different. And, it might be noted, Hawaiians of the past and many Hawaiians today are unaware that others do—or even can—perceive things without perceiving them as conscious and related to them as kin.[18]

It was said in the Preface that most Hawaiians today don't learn the traditional philosophy as it is described in these pages. Yet they approach the world in a Hawaiian way that fits hand-in-glove with the philosophy. Hawaiian philosophy mirrors a centuries-old approach to life which cannot be expunged from the culture. The Hawaiian who aches for the land as he watches Westerners—and now the Asians—buy it up and pave it over may not be able to say

how he is related to the land, but he knows that he is in his bones. The Hawaiian who puts his life on the line standing in front of a bulldozer may not know why he must defend the land in that way, but he cannot turn away. With or without the philosophical tradition, the Hawaiian knows that he forms a community with nature around him. Nature constantly and faithfully consciously provides for and protects him. And he is compelled from deep within to protect nature in turn. And he does this with the same courage and bravery a non-Hawaiian summons to defend **his** family and community from an aggressor.

Modern Corroboration
Of Sentience In Nature

THE QUESTION OF whether non-human beings of the cosmic community actually are cognizant deserves some discussion.

Although in modern times, Westerners by and large think of the cosmos as insentient, this view was introduced only in the seventeenth century. From before the time of the Greek philosopher Thales, who lived in the sixth century before Christ, until the time of the French philosopher Descartes, sixteen hundred years after Christ, most Western men of learning thought that nature was alive and, at least loosely speaking, conscious.[1] Descartes changed all this with his new interpretation of the nature of man's body and soul, and how they work together. He wrote that it is man's soul (or spirit or *ego* or mind) alone which thinks. Man's material body is totally incapable of thinking or knowing or sensing. Descartes' followers further developed this idea to apply to the whole universe, contending that all of material nature was insentient. In doing so, they destroyed the thought foundation that supported the mutually protective, consciously interacting relationship between Western man and the non-human beings of the cosmos, and they created a cleavage between man and nature which has never since been bridged. Following this precedent, over the centuries, Western man generally has further developed only the view of matter as unknowing and inert.

Westerners, however, are not the only ones to venture opinions on the sentience or insentience of nature. One finds that many non-Western peoples are prepared by their religious and philosophical world-views to accept nature as in one way or another possessing an underlying consciousness. In the Hindu thought of India, it is taught that all observable matter is underlain by Brahman, the one, thinking, planning, acting, and animating Divine Reality. The universe and all that is in it are not "many things," but rather are the many varied forms in which Brahman makes Himself observably present. And since all of nature is Brahman, all of nature itself, as Brahman, is conscious.

The great classical literature of China also addresses the relationship and interaction of humans and nature. The *Tao Te Ching* speaks of the *Tao* as that from which all comes. All the things of the universe are "of the same nature" as this ultimate source from which they derive. It is by bringing one's actions into harmony with one's true nature (*Tao*) deep within one's being that one can flow along in harmony with the rest of nature. In ancient days, natural calamities and disasters were thought to come about because humans were out of sync with the flow of nature. It was the role of the sage-king to maintain the harmony of the universe by leading his people to conform their actions to the way of nature—so that heaven, earth, and humans would continue to flow along together harmoniously. In general, Chinese thought shies away from attributing consciousness to *Tao*, and from pointing to the *Tao* as "consciousness" underlying nature. But it does speak of a "Will of Heaven" that brings about calamities when things are out of sync with the *Tao*. Chinese tradition seems to credit this "Will of Heaven" with the kind of determinative action that we associate with consciousness.

Zen is a Japanese school of mysticism. In Zen the aspirant strives for oneness with Being itself. In pursuing this end he meditates, seeking a kind of mystic transformation into nature during which he will experience nature "as nature experiences itself." This whole endeavor also is based on the presumption that nature experiences.

In the centuries since Descartes, the West has not been totally devoid of great thinkers who have developed the concept of consciousness in nature. Hegel, Shopenhauer, Fichte, Shelling, Bergson, Heidegger, and Whitehead are but a few of the philosophers who have in various ways made significant contributions to the discussion.

Pierre Teilhard de Chardin stands out among modern theologians. This Jesuit palaeontologist-theologian, who profoundly influenced Catholic and non-Catholic Christians, was clearly inspired by the mystic tradition of China where he worked for many decades. Teilhard de Chardin viewed God as a being who indwells and animates all of nature. For him, everything in the cosmos is alive and conscious and able to interrelate with man, because the all-knowing and relating God indwells all of natural being. God can be recognized and worshipped in the myriad forms of nature, and even enjoyed in mystic oneness with nature.

Despite this great body of world thought supporting conciousness in nature, the effect of Descartes' philosophy has been so pervasive that few Westerners today are willing to even entertain the idea of a sentient cosmos. In many circles one would fear the loss of his credibility should he discuss the subject seriously.

It is surprising, then, that modern science itself is now attempting to break through this prejudice. Over the last decade there have been a number of documentaries and articles in scientific journals describing experiments with consciousness in lower species.

In discussing the question here, a sampling of material from the scientific community is presented. Our intent is not to attempt to establish that the concept of a conscious cosmos is correct. Rather, being concerned that the concept is too easily dismissed as the fancy of a primitive people, our purpose is to draw attention to scientific work going on in this area and to some conclusions of contemporary scientists.

A good place to start looking at kinds of conscious activity—such as thinking and willing—in nature might be in survival methods. Living beings need nourishment to survive, and many hunt and kill in order to eat. It is difficult to deny that thinking is going on when an animal hunts, stalks, and then challenges and fights its prey to death. Through the ages this process has been ascribed to instinct: "An animal is hungry; its instinct tells it to kill and eat; and it does." But this explanation is not sufficient: too much of the process demands a complex processing of information. Searching for food when hunger strikes may be instinct. Looking for a certain food may also be. But the hunting and killing demands thinking. It demands familiarity with the animal's own surroundings, and knowing the likely haunts of its prey. Many animals, such as sharks and lions, pick a particular individual from a group or herd, and pass up others within easier reach in pursuing the one selected. Making such choices seems to require at least a rudimentary weighing of distinctions between possible prey, and a decision in selecting one victim. Stalking and attacking require dependence on remembered facts learned through experience, in order to anticipate and counter escape tactics. Life and death battles are not programmed. They require very quick, complex thought.

Some animals are particularly interesting for their successful counter-moves and evasive techniques. Some moths, for example, have learned the meaning of the sonar sound emitted by bats. And when they hear that high screech honed in on them, they stop dead in mid-air, letting gravity draw them below the path of the swooping bat. While it might be argued that this has become an instinctual, reflexive move, it is possible that each generation learns the process from older peer moths. And even if this technique has become an instinctive act, it certainly was not such among the first generation of moths that practiced it. Look at the learning process involved. Bats were successful at locating and swallowing moths in flight until one or more moths recognized the bat as a major consumer of its fellows, identified the ultra-sonic screech with the bat, realized the connection between the ultra-sonics directed at prey and the swift arrival of the bat, and either by experiment or by accident discovered the successful freezing of action and falling out of the bat's path. Thought was involved throughout this process. Passing the technique on involved communication, teaching, and learning. If the discovering moth had no way to pass on his information, the evasive technique would have been lost when the moth died. And if other moths learned it by observation, their learning involved thinking (observation and comparison) and willing in the adoption of the technique for themselves.

Prairie dogs farm. Other animals use tools. A heron (bird) living at the Miami Seaquarium is the subject of an article in a *National Geographic Magazine*. The bird has learned to fish, a skill not thought to be common to its species. Food pellets are sold in a vending machine so that Seaquarium visitors may feed the fish. The heron picks up a pellet, takes it to the water, drops it in, lies in wait till a fish comes up for it, and then grabs the fish with its beak. If a fish does not come soon enough, the heron will take the pellet to another area of the park and repeat the process. Since other members of this heron's family now also fish, it is thought that after learning the skill himself, this heron taught it to the others.[2]

E.I. Mukhin, a Russian scientist, in work at the USSR Academy of Medical Science, claims to have "shown that cats are not only capable of concrete mental activity, but that 'abstract thinking' is also possible."[3]

Migrating birds are some of the most extraordinary thinking animals. Flying thousands of miles—sometimes, like the plover, over open ocean with no navigational cues but the sun and stars—they make their expected landfall, often returning to the same branch of the same tree year after year. Although storms may force migrating birds hundreds of miles off course, their compensating navigational ability allows most to reach their intended destination.[4] Stephen T. Emlen of Cornell University, using indigo buntings (which are night migrants), showed that his birds depended on stars in the northern part of the sky, and that they need not see all of them in order to orient successfully.[5] He showed that "their ability was acquired, not inborn. At first, young buntings determined the north-south axis by rotation of the stars, but soon learned to determine direction by star patterns."

Birds have some sensory powers that far exceed man's: their vision is acute; some see polarized and ultraviolet light as well as color; some hear infrasound—noise in ultralow frequencies of long wavelength that may carry for a thousand miles or more in the atmosphere; and some sense the earth's magnetic field and read direction by that additional sense.[6] For migrating birds that find their direction primarily through celestial navigation, these greater sensing abilities make the information which they must synthesize in their piloting judgements quite complex.

A possible conclusion from this cursory look at the animal world may be found in an article by Donald Griffin in the journal *Behavioral and Brain Sciences*:

> Ethologists and comparative psychologists have found that the social behavior, discrimination learning, and especially the communicative behavior of many animals are sufficiently versatile to call into question the customary denial that animals have mental experiences comparable to those of humans. Many animal behavior patterns suggest that they have mental images of objects, events, or relationships remote from the immediate stimulus situation, as well as self-awareness and intentions concerning future actions.[7]

Perhaps in the future it will be thought that Descartes and those who followed him did Western man a disservice by causing him to sever his relationship with a sentient, cosmic community around him. Perhaps one day it will be seen that Western man has for centuries put up barriers to developing a meaningful relationship with the greater part of his possible realm of experience.

**Exploring the Concept of
A Consciously Evolving Cosmos**

Conscious activity possibly may also be traceable in the planning and effecting of evolutionary advance. A study of the notion of conscious evolution might start with the beginning of the universe. Most scientists agree that our universe began with an explosion called the "Big Bang." They suggest that a "primordial soup," composed of sub-atomic particles, existed before the Big Bang. The Big Bang forged the sub-atomic particles into atoms, producing the atomic structure which is now common to everything in the universe. Science, however, limits itself to study of areas for which there can be replicated experimentation. Thus, most scientists are unwilling to publicly speculate about what caused the Big Bang. Saying they cannot know, they leave answering that question to philosophers and men of religion. What did cause the Big Bang? Was it an accident? Was it caused by an outside agent? Or was it the result of a plan for evolutionary advance, a conscious make-it-or-break-it gamble by the entire sentient sub-atomic community?[8]

Other than sheer conjecture, is there any reason to think that matter on the sub-atomic level is conscious? Or is the behavior of sub-atomic particles completely mechanistic and predictable? Scientists have no explanation for the behavior of photons—the sub-atomic light forces which appear randomly and cause electrons to jump from one orbit around the nucleus to another. Atomic theory says that atoms by nature remain in their lowest energy state, in which case all electrons should remain in their regular orbits. Photons appear irregularly and unpredictably. Their light added to an electron causes an energy change which precipitates the orbital jump. Attempts to calculate how often, how many, or where photons will appear have not been successful. Such random, unpredictable behavior should not be possible if atomic function is purely mechanistic.[9]

On the molecular level, gas molecules present another non-deterministic situation for physicists studying the fundamental building blocks of nature. It is impossible to predict the motion of molecules in the air we breathe or in any other gas. Again, if molecules are purely mechanistic, the motion of each molecule should be predictable.

In Hawaiian thought the material universe is conscious. Its actions are caused from within. It is interesting to apply that view to evolutionary activity in the atomic and molecular realms. Atoms evolve to the more complex "molecules" by uniting with other suitable atoms (atoms with proper valence). Simple molecules then bond with other molecules in evolving to complex molecules. According to Darwinian evolutionary theory, this upward movement to greater complexity would be explained as blind a groping by atoms and molecules whose nature it is to tend towards higher forms. Applying "sentient" notions, it would be explained as activity similar to that going on in human life: the first stable union is made either by accident or experimentation, that success is communicated to all the rest of the species, and the move to molecular existence and then mega-molecular existence is undertaken because it is seen by the whole community as advantageous and fulfilling. The cause of evolutionary progress in such a sentient cosmos might be the desire of species to expand their realms of possible experience for themselves and their progeny.

Further exploring the concept of a consciously evolving cosmos: in David Attenborough's thirteen-part television series, *Life On Earth: A Natural History* (produced by the BBC and shown on public television in the United States in 1982), the history of evolution was presented as a series of innovations which various species caused in their own forms in order master situations they encountered. For example, "It was in order to drag themselves up onto the shore that fishes developed legs from fins."[10] Birds originally had tiny teeth along their jaws, but teeth added too greatly to their weight, so they developed the lighter beak to aid their flying.[11] Bats developed sonar in order to "see" in the dark.[12] Iguanas in the South American forests lived in trees and fed on leaves, but when they reached the Galapagos Islands they fed on seaweed, so they developed unusually long claws in order to hold onto rocks when the waves crashed over them.[13]

Animals developed color to add to their attractiveness in winning mates. They also used color for protection. The viceroy butterfly did not itself taste bad, but it developed a pattern and coloring very close to that of the terrible-tasting monarch butterfly so that predators would mistake it for the monarch and leave it alone.

Warm-blooded mammals had to eat more than cold blooded animals in order to stay warm. They developed grinder teeth to chew things, which would hurry the digestion. They also developed body hair to retain their heat.[14]

Perhaps the most important evidence of conscious planning of evolution throughout nature is found in flowering plants and in their relationships with insects and birds. In the segment, "The Devouring Hoards: Insects," David Attenborough discusses at length the way that plants have used insects to assist in their reproduction, and how they have developed their flowers in ways to help recruit the insects. He states that many flowers contain both male and female reproductive cells and have the potential for self-fertilization. But when pollen—the substance plants use for fertilization—is brought to a female reproductive cell from a different plant of the same species, it results in variation in offspring, rather than offspring identical to the one parent plant. The greater the variation within a species, the greater the opportunities for further evolution: variation is the raw material of evolution. Plants learned that insects and birds ate their pollen, but that they did not eat it all. Further, plants found that insects were messy eaters and got the pollen they were eating all over their bodies. When these insects would later visit other plants of the same species, looking for more pollen to eat, they would frequently brush off the pollen collected on their bodies from the earlier plant, thus fertilizing the second plant with pollen from the first, and causing the desired greater variation in offspring. "As pollen munching by insects began to spread, plants produced more pollen than they needed for fertilization, and all kinds of insects visited their flowers to feed on it." As time went on, flowers produced sweet-tasting nectar for their pollen-transporting birds and insects to eat. Then they developed colors, even brilliant colors that could be seen at a distance, to alert insects to the presence of their fine tasting nectar. They also developed perfumes to summon insects. Some plants developed patterns on their flowers which were instructions to the insects, showing them where to land and exactly where to look for pollen and nectar. Some of these plants developed their designs and instructions within the same color range of the spectrum seen by humans because the animals they wished to attract saw colors within that range. Other plants, however, developed their informational patterns in ultra-violet in order to communicate instructions to insects that saw in ultra-violet.[15]

A quite striking example of the interdevelopment of a plant and an insect is found with a species in the orchid family and the ignumen wasp (the insect species which transports the orchid's pollen). The orchid developed not only a perfume like that produced by the female ignumen wasp, but also an appearance so similar to the female wasp that the male ignumen wasp mistakes the flower for a mate and copulates with the flower. The orchid's pollen is so placed on the bloom that it sticks to the abdomen of the wasp while it is copulating. Then when the wasp goes to copulate with the next flower, it delivers the pollen it picked up while mating with the first flower.[16]

This orchid is totally dependent on this one species of ignumen wasp for its pollenation and, therefore, its survival. The orchid can only survive as long as the ignumen wasp does. There are a number of other species in nature which have developed exclusive relationships such as this. A considerable portion of the thirteen hour series, *Life On Earth*, is given to showing examples of how plants and animals have evolved together in intricate ways so that they can have the exclusive rights to, and services of, the other.

Conclusions That Might Be Drawn About "Knowing" in Nature

If one allows that minerals, plants, and animals can plan and effect their own evolutionary development, some points can be made. These plants have no brains. They also have no senses. The orchid just mentioned developed a flower that looked so much like the female ignumen wasp that the male wasp performed as though it were. Yet the orchid had no eye to see the model insect, nor nose to smell its scent, nor brain to plan the development of its flower and smell. The orchid developed color and form for the insect to "see." Yet, not having eyes itself, it could not know what "to see" even meant. If indeed, then, the plant itself brought about its own development, this argues for an exceptional knowing ability comprehending things beyond its capabilities for experience.

Telepathy and clairvoyance are possibly the comparative knowing abilities in man. A human ordinarily knows only what his senses—eyes, ears, nose, taste, and touch—can inform him of. When, through extra-sensory perception, he knows the thoughts that others are thinking (telepathy), or even more, when he knows and shares the experiences of a person in another place (clairvoyance), these ways of knowing things beyond his experience seem similar to the mode of knowing that we have observed in plants.

Should one ever reach the point where he could totally experience the experience of another, or totally experience "the mountain as the mountain" as Zen masters would have us do, he could then perhaps understand how a plant could develop a flower for an insect to see, when the plant itself could not physically experience seeing.

If nature is cognizant, and if the kind of knowledge-gathering done by the orchid and by other lower beings which do not have senses is seemingly the same kind of knowledge-gathering which in man we call extra-sensory perception, then perhaps extra-sensory perception, rather than the discursive thought common to humans, is nature's basic mode of knowing.

It has not been the intent of this chapter to establish that nature is sentient or that evolutionary advance is indeed planned and executed from within. It has shown, however, that modern science is investigating views which the ancient Hawaiians developed, and since this is true, there should be no shame in proposing that the Hawaiian world-view be given serious consideration by thinking people in the modern world.

Akua, Mana, And Divinity

Degree of *Mana* the Mark of Divinity

AKUA HAS BEEN TRANSLATED repeatedly as "sentient spirit" or "spirit consciousness." What does it have to do with divinity? The distinction between common *akua* and divine *akua* seems to be that the divine *akua* has a greater amount of *mana* (spiritual power). This accounts for the phenomenon that chiefs could also claim divinity while they were living and reigning. They clearly were seen to be human—to have virtues and failings, physical strengths and weaknesses; they could be wounded in battle or killed; and the people would overthrow them if they were tyrannical, divine though they were. What made them different—made them divine—was the *mana* with which they were born because of their blood line and genealogical standing and because of the circumstances surrounding their birth.

That *mana* was the distinguishing factor is stated by both Kepelino and Malo. Kepelino writes,

> "These ruling chiefs were put into the class of gods because of the great power (*mana*) they had and the *tapu* observed toward them....The chiefs were called "gods that could be seen." They were held in high esteem in Hawaii, adored and so forth or sometimes worshipped."[1]

And Malo supports this:

> "The *ali'i nui* was exalted and worshipped because he had great *mana*; like a god was his *mana. E kiekie ai ka alii,*

e hoomana ia no, no ka mea, ua mana nui ia na alii nui ua like me ke akua ka mana."[2]

All *akua* were thought to be the same in fundamental nature. The *akua* in a tree or a shark or a human was not different from a high god. Two things that did set them apart were: first, the lower species were limited by functional constraints on their knowing powers which were determined by the physical form they indwelt, and second, the divine spirit had more *mana*, which enhanced his capabilities for knowing and acting. Again there was no "Supreme Being" or "Creator" god concept in Hawaii. "Gods" were the souls of deceased humans which had been empowered with great *mana*.

The Abilities of the Soul after Death

To more clearly understand the distinction between gods and humans, it will be helpful to discuss Hawaiian ideas about the soul (*akua*) freed by death from the constraints of the body.

The Hawaiian word for the soul is *'uhane*. The soul (*'uhane*) of man is an *akua*.[3] After death the *'uhane* was thought to keep many of the human characteristics it had in life. It was thought to go about in the shape of a body.[4] It shivered in the cold[5] and could be hungry and thirsty. Bodies were buried with food, eating bowls, *kapa*, spears, hatchets, and so forth because it was thought that they used those things in the place of the afterlife.[6] The *akua* consumed essences of the food it was offered and used the essences of implements with which it was buried.

The spirit was thought to keep its reasoning powers, its memory, and its emotions. It could retain an interest in family affairs and could continue both to love those it had loved in life and to dislike those it had disliked.[7]

Like all *akua* indwelling species of nature, from conception[8] the *'uhane* had assumed the limitations determined by the physical form of the species it had entered. But once separated from the dead human body and freed of its constraints, the soul was no longer bound by laws of extension: it could be large or very small.[9] It could transport itself from place to place very rapidly.[10] It could also again be in several places at one time.[11] So its knowledge was more extensive and better informed.[12] Since after death a soul's use of its extra-sensory perception (*'ike pāpālua*) also was again unrestrained, it could know the thoughts of others (telepathy), know the presence of things in other places (clairvoyance), know the future (precognition), and exercise power over matter in various ways (psychokinesis). Its knowledge was still somewhat localized, however. Hawaiians did not attribute cosmic knowledge to spirits.

The *'uhane* could take other forms: it could assume forms of animals, plants, minerals, or meteorological phenomena at will.[13] If the soul was accepted by an ancestral god (*'aumakua*) who indwelt some nature form, like a shark or a bird, and if it went to dwell in that realm, it was given the nature-form of that divinity.[14] The soul could dwell in several forms at the same time.

In continuing its relationship with humans, a spirit might reappear in its ghostly form for some time after death. It could communicate with the living through mediums.[15] The *'uhane* could "perch" on living people for a time to inspire them,[16] or it could totally possess them. Possession was always temporary and could be for good as well as for bad.[17] Finally, a spirit could also join the several spirits (*kino akua*) that comprised the guiding self (the higher spirit group composing the mind) of a living person: it might remain there permanently, acting as an indwelling guide or protector, and becoming an actual part of the self.[18]

The Polynesian Gods Are Ancestral Spirits

Among the early Polynesians, "gods" were no more than, or different from, powerful ancestral spirits who would help man when called upon. Polynesia has a long tradition of praying to ancestors for aid. The practice is found in Tonga[19] and Sāmoa[20] —the first-settled Polynesian islands— and likely can be traced back to the original Austronesians and beyond.

That the high gods of the Polynesians were only human ancestors can be determined by an examination of the religious traditions in Easter Island and Mangareva. Both places were settled from the Marquesas very early, before the Marquesans became the first to settle Hawai'i. It is likely that Easter Island and Mangareva were both settled by only one voyaging canoe of people, the settlers then losing contact with the rest of Polynesia. So the religious ideas they share with each other very likely reflect those of earliest Polynesia. On each island, the names of the four great gods worshiped in most of Polynesia—and in Hawai'i—are known, but they are known only as legendary figures or divine ancestors heading genealogies.[21] It can be argued, then, that the people from the Marquesas who first settled Hawai'i in the early first millenium brought with them a small group of traditional ancestral spirits or gods, and also brought the practice of praying to these deceased ancestors.

Ho'omanamana Deification: A Hawaiian Innovation:

Deification, as commonly thought of, is a proclamation by people living on earth that a deceased soul has been received into, or advanced to, the status of "divinity." While the proclamation is made on earth, the actual change of the soul from human to divine is thought to occur wherever the soul is, in the place of the afterlife. For example, in Tonga and Sāmoa the souls of chiefs were said to go to different heavens from the commoners.[22] When they were believed to have arrived there, they were proclaimed gods by the people living on earth.

Deification in ancient Hawai'i differed from this in that the entire change took place on earth, at the place where the corpse lay, and while the ritual was taking place. Further, it was not simply a proclamation of a deification; the ritual was the cause of the change. Except for the few ancestral spirits they initially brought with them, the Hawaiians themselves created all of their gods.

There were a variety of ideas about what **ordinarily** happened to the spirit after death, where it went, and what the place of the afterlife was like. One of the most common was that its *'aumākua*, its ancestral spirits, met the soul as it left the body. Since the soul initially was quite weak, they nourished it for a period of days. When it was strong enough, they led it to the *leina*, the leaping place from which it leapt into the place of the afterlife. There was a wide variety of ideas on what existence was like in the place of the afterlife. None of them were very inviting. Emerson, for instance, gives this description:

> This was an insubstantial land of twilight and shades, a
> barren and waterless waste, unblest by grass, or flower,

or tree, or growing herb. Here the famished ghosts of
men...fled each other's presence in fear and suspicion.[23]

Wishing to keep a loved spirit close by, where it could be
called upon to help the living, the Hawaiians developed a
mode of deification which took advantage of the initial
weakness of the spirit, its need for nourishment, and its fear
of that unknown, possibly bleak place of the afterlife.

Spirits of the deceased retained an attachment to, and
identity with, their bones. So, after death, while the spirit
was still weak and hovering around the place of death, the
body was baked until the flesh separated from the bones.
Then the bones were cleaned and put into a bundle (*pu'olo*)
or a woven casket. The spirit was then encouraged to return
into the bones where it could have a permanent home in
familiar surroundings. It was offered food and drink and
promised daily feeding. There were then prayers imparting
mana (spiritual power) to the spirit. If the spirit entered the
bones again, daily feeding and imparting *mana* through
prayer enabled it to become a powerful *akua* who could be
called upon (commanded) to protect and help its
keeper—the one who fed it—and others who had a right to
call upon it. This spirit called back into its bones and deified
in this way was called an *'unihipili*.[24]

Ho'omanamana, the imparting of *mana*, was the core of the
deification practice. The way to raise a spirit to divine status
was to give it greater *mana*. J.S. Emerson comments:

> Let me here distinctly remark that the worship
> (*hoomanamana*) rendered to the spirit is not an ascription
> of power already possessed by the object worshipped, but
> an imparting to it of *mana* (power) which, but for this
> worship, it would never have. In short, the god does not
> make the *kahuna* (priest), but the *kahuna* often makes his
> god.[25]

The process of making an *'unihipili* was practiced by both commoners and chiefs. But when a chief died, there were more elaborate rituals for his deification. These added the requisite degree of *mana* to his discarnate spirit (*akua*) to elevate him to full divinity. A service for an *ali'i nui*, described by Malo, reinforces the role of *mana* in the deification:

> "His bones were taken and he was en-mana-ed into a god. (He was 'caused *mana*' or given *mana* until he was a god.)
> *E lawe ia kona mau iwi a hoomana ia ia i akua."*

> "His bones were taken into divinity and they were prayed into by the *kahuna mua.*
> *A lawe ia ua mau iwi la i akua a pule ia e na kahuna mua."*

> "The deification of the dead king being accomplished, he was worshipped as a real god.

> "Those bones, then, were permanently absorbed into *ho'omanamana* divinity, and he **was** an ancestral god."
> *A laila lilo loa ua mau iwi la i akua hoomana ia, ua kapa ia kona inoa he akua aumakua.*[26]

The *ho'omanamana* genre of deification is an Hawaiian innovation. It is based upon several underlying principles, all of which represent distinctions in traditional Polynesian thought made by the Hawaiians.[27] The first of these is that divinities are the same in nature as all other spirit consciousnesses (*akua*) found throughout the cosmos. The second is that *mana* is the enhancing power that enables *akua* to perform in a preternatural or supernatural manner. With the fullness of *mana* comes extensive knowledge, wider-ranging precognition, teleportation, control over matter, and greater ability to assume multiple forms. The third is that what distinguishes divinities from other *akua* is the amount of *mana* they possess. The fourth is that *mana* is a body of spiritual power which may be drawn upon and directed by those with the right or "gift" to do so. And the fifth is that *mana* can be transferred into the possession or control of others, such as a deified spirit ('*unihipili*).

Akua Mana and Akua Ho'omanamana

In Hawai'i the way that a god acquired his *mana* became the differentiating characteristic among the gods: the ancient gods who were brought in the first immigration from the Marquesas were called *akua mana*, gods already possessing *mana*. Those deified by the Hawaiians were called *akua ho'omanamana*, "gods caused to have *mana*."

The high gods, Kāne, Kū, Lono, Kanaloa, and Hina, were not thought to differ in fundamental nature from the *ho'omanamana* gods. Over the centuries a large number of myths, some of which contradicted others, were associated with their names. Overlapping realms of responsibility were also ascribed to them, and their personages became very complex. But there was never anything in the conception of the high gods which required that they be any more than spirit consciousnesses, *akua*, freed of all bodily constraints, who had very great *mana*.

Kino Lau: Assuming Multiple Forms

HAWAIIANS BELIEVED that spirits had the ability to assume multiple forms or multiple bodies (*kino lau*). Among the *kino lau* an *akua* could assume were human, animal, plant, or mineral forms, the forms of meteorological phenomena, and even action forms.[1]

Kino lau is illustrated by the forms that the goddess Hina takes in the *Kumulipo*.[2] According to one story in the chant, Hina, in her spirit form, notices the human, Akalana, and becomes enamoured with his physical attributes. She assumes a human form to become his lover, or wife, and gives birth to their child, Maui. In this part of the story she is called Hina-in-the-fire. Later in the story she appears as a mudhen. She also is called Hina-ke-ka, which refers to the form Hina takes as a scoop for bailing water out of a canoe. Within this one section, then, Hina is seen as a spirit, a human, a mudhen, fire, and a canoe bailer. In another place it is stated that the great mother goddess, Haumea, is another form of Hina. And the *Kumulipo* says that Haumea has "four-hundred-thousand forms, and four thousand more forms, and yet thousands and thousands of forms."[3]

In Hawaiian thought, every spirit can have more than one instantiation: that is, every spirit, every *akua*, has the potentiality to take form in more than one place at one time. While all spirits—either of the living or of the dead—can assume at least some other forms,[4] the higher gods are believed to manifest themselves in almost unlimited numbers of things at the same time. So many are the species said to be *kino lau* of one major god or another that Handy was led to write: "probably if we knew in its entirety the ancient Hawaiian teachings about nature and creation, it would be found that every natural phenomenon and form of life was thought to be an embodiment of a particular god or demigod."[5]

The idea that the spirit of a deceased person could enter other natural forms was quite common in much of Polynesia. It served as an explanation for how a dead chief could go to dwell in a star, for instance, for how he could "be" the star and be worshiped "as" the star. The ancient Hawaiians took that simple Polynesian idea, that spirits of the dead could go into other natural forms, and developed it into the great theological system of *kino lau* (many forms). Which species of nature the various major gods indwelt was clearly designated, even though there might be overlap. When Captain Cook arrived, people throughout the Hawaiian islands commonly perceived and revered the gods as existing in generally the same forms of nature. (Cook was the first European known to have located the Hawaiian islands. He arrived in 1778. Later references in this book to pre-Cook and post-Cook Hawai'i use his arrival to point up the beginning of Western influence in the islands.)

Kino Lau Possibly Developed by the Mystic Schools

The concept of *kino lau* is not consistent with the evolutionary development of the *Kumulipo*. The *Kumulipo* makes no mention of "the high gods" inhabiting the species of nature as they evolved. It speaks only of simple *akua* entering species: "*akua*, having no human characteristics." According to the *Kumulipo*'s schema of evolution, the high gods were born in the eighth *wā*, after all of nature was complete, and man and woman were on the scene. This would be logical if man created his gods.

How did the gods, then, get projected back into the forms of nature? There were different theological schools and traditions in ancient Hawai'i. It is this writer's opinion that the system of kino lau grew out of another school, one different from that which devised the evolutionary schema of the *Kumulipo*. This was a school of mysticism.

There is no doubt that the deeper forms of prayer were known and practiced in ancient Hawai'i. David Malo writes of the ecstatic love some experienced in prayer.[6] There are Hawaiian words for meditation and contemplation. And there are *heiaus* which are known to have been used for meditative prayer.[7] The use, during prayer, of 'awa, a calming drink which produced pseudo-mystical effects— causing one to forget the cares of the world and to concentrate deeply on one thought—was a natural preparation for and introduction to mysticism.

The experience of mystic union is the same as the "oneness with the beloved" that a person who is deeply in love enjoys when he is lifted into the rapture of ecstasy. In the ecstatic experience the lover becomes oblivious of the world around him and oblivious of time, much as happens in a daydream. He moves into another realm, another dimension, a different experience of reality. Time and his ordinary world seem to exist separately from him. As he ascends the heights of ecstasy, he also loses consciousness even of his own individuality. Losing himself completely in love, and no longer aware of differentiations between himself and the rest of reality, he and his beloved become one. The same happens in the mystic experience: all separations fall away and the devotee becomes immersed in oneness, oneness with all being...some say with divine being.

The Hawaiian experienced this mystic oneness with his gods and with all of reality around him. Perhaps in one mystic tradition, priests who had known mystical oneness—the unity of themselves, the divine, and nature—needed to reconcile their experience with their tradition of multiple gods. Having experienced themselves and their gods as one with nature, they took the theory that spirits could dwell in great numbers of forms at the same time, and began to attribute the presences of the major gods and goddesses—Kū, Kāne, Lono, Kanaloa, Hina, and Haumea—to various natural forms, loving them and enjoying their return of love in this form and that.

One finds such an experience in the long Kāne litany given by Martha Beckwith. One can see the mystic— standing, enthralled with nature and filled with love, calling out to his god, Kāne, whom he experiences in this cloud, then that cloud, and then another. The mystic even blends the gods together in his unitive experience: He begins, "O Kāne-Kanaloa," naming the two gods as if they were one. He further blurs the distinction between the gods in that most of the areas in which he experiences Kāne in this prayer are cloud forms traditionally thought of as forms of the god Lono. The litany begins:

O Kane-Kanaloa!
O Kane of the great lightning flashes in the heavens
O Kane the render of heaven
O Kane the rolling stone
O Kane of the whirlwind
O Kane of the rainbow
O Kane of the atmosphere
O Kane of the rain
O Kane of the heavenly cloud
O Kane standing before the pointed clouds
O Kane standing before the heavenly clouds
O Kane in the cloud above
O Kane in the cloud floating low
O Kane in the cloud resting on the summit
O Kane in the cloud over the low hills
O Kane of the heavenly star
O Kane of the dawn
O Kane of the clouds on the horizon
O Kane of the red rainbow
O Kane of the great wind
O Kane of the little wind
O Kane of the zephyrs
O Kane of the peaceful breeze
O Kane of the great thrust....[8]

As time went on, the belief that gods inhabited many forms of nature was incorporated into the beliefs surrounding *'unihipili* deification of chiefs. This is seen in the chant *"He Kanikau No Pe'ape'a"*:

Beloved Ka-lani who passed away	*Aloha ka-lani i hele aku nei,*
The body of the chief was baked	*Ua ahi ka-lani*
The flesh was separated	*Ua momoku ka ili*
Ka-lani took on an akua body	*Ua mea e ka lani, ua kino akua,*
He became many bodies, many transfigured forms.	*Ua kino lau, kino lau pahaohao*
The body of the chief burst forth into divinity	*Ua haona ke kino o ka lani i ke akua.*
Ka-lani became a new god	*Ka lani, akua hou*

of Koolau	*o Koolau*
He returned to the calmness of	*I hoi i ka lulu o*
Kapueokahi (at Hana, Maui)...	*Kapueokahi...*
To the many living at the beach of	*Ke kini noho kahakai o*
Nanualele (also at Hana, Maui).	*Nanualele.*[9]

It might be asked where the new forms came from when spirits assumed other forms. There seem to have been three different answers, three different modes or methods of transformation. When a spirit such as that of the just mentioned chief, Kalani, assumed another form, his spirit indwelt an already existing form. In other instances the process seemed to involve "shifting" from one form to another. For instance, Kamapua'a appeared frequently as a handsome young man and then shifted his form to that of a pig simply by willing it. In yet other cases the new form seems to have been materialized from nothing, such as when *'aumākua* (ancestral gods) on occasion fashioned material forms for themselves such as a rainbow, a lizard, a hawk, or a fish, in order to appear in warning or as a sign of reassurance or good luck.

The Role of *Kino Lau* in Forming Familial Ties between Man and Nature

There was a form of deification which involved the theory of form transformation. If a family of fishermen had no close ties to a shark *'aumakua* (ancestral god) who might protect them from other sharks while they were out fishing, *kākū'ai* deification was a practice by which they might strengthen their familial ties in the shark world. They would take the body of a just-deceased family member to the *kahu* (priest or keeper) of one of the great shark gods, asking to have the deceased "assumed into" that shark god. The shark god would be summoned by its *kahu* and, if the god was seen to be willing to accept the family as closely related *'ohana* (family), the body, wrapped in a cloth with clearly recognizable markings, would be placed in the water beside the shark. The shark god would then accept the spirit of the deceased into oneness with himself and come into the body. Over a period of a few weeks, while the *kahu* continued feeding and making offerings to the god, the body would take on the shape of a shark. The new shark would be another form, a *kino lau*, of that shark god. This family, being now as closely related to the shark god as they had been to the deceased, would recognize the relative at sea by its markings which were the same as those on the cloth in which the corpse was wrapped. They would then have a claim on him when in need of protection. This form of deification was called *kākū'ai*.

Kino lau played another important role in explaining how one could be related as family to nature forms. If a god who most commonly dwelt in a particular animal, plant, or mineral took on a human form and had sexual relations with a woman, their descendants would trace their lineage to the god in the animal, plant, or mineral form he usually inhabited and would be related to that entire species of animal, plant, or mineral.

To summarize the ways one might be related to nature, then, one might be related as family through direct evolutionary descent, as the *Kumulipo* showed all humans were. If one could trace direct descent in his genalogy from one of the high gods, he would be further related to all of the *kino lau* which that god assumed. If one were descended from a god who ordinarily dwelt in a nature-form but who had taken human-form to mate with a woman, the descendant would be related to the nature form of his ancestor. If one had an ancestor who at death had assumed some natural form—either like a chief going into a star, or like a person deified through *kākuʻai* being assumed into a shark god or some other form of nature—that person was also related to the nature form of that ancestor.

Because of his belief in *kino lau*, the Hawaiian who today practices the traditional religion, when looking at a mountain, feels his relationship to his god Kū in that mountain form. Looking at the sun, he views a presence of his god, Kāne, and experiences the god's warmth on his body. The cloud forms are Lono. And the sea is Kanaloa. Many trees, plants, and animals are other *kino lau* of the gods. The presences of the gods around him give the Hawaiian a constant sense of religious encounter. Nature is not only conscious, much of it is divine. And as he interrelates with and interacts with nature, he interrelates and interacts with the gods.

Many other Hawaiians who now practice Christianity still know the animal and plant species to which they are most closely related, and they feel a special tie as family with them. Many times one hears Hawaiians make references to their *ʻaumākua* in conversation: comments like, "And then I saw the rainbow and knew....When I heard the owl, I....Our family is related to Pele, so....I'm not afraid of sharks because...."

Many, if not most, Hawaiians still have a general orientation in which they experience all of nature as distantly related kin. They have a sense of familial belonging in a world that is not made up of cold, inert objects, but rather of warm, conscious beings, many of whom can be called upon for assistance, guidance, and reassurance.

A Correct Perception of Hawaiian Religion

The differences between Hawaiian and Western perspectives on divinity sometimes cause unwarranted fear of, and disrespect for, the Hawaiian gods. Christians, brought up with ideas that heaven is above and hell is below, and that white symbolizes goodness, virtue, and divinity, while black symbolizes the devil and evil, sometimes look askance at the Hawaiian for his worship of beings dwelling in the underworld and for his reverence of the black or darkness. In this day of space exploration, it has become obvious that heaven is not above the clouds, and what is below is not hell but the other side of the world. Nevertheless, it is important to note that Hawaiians practicing the ancient religion have never prayed to gods who reside "in the realm of the devil." Just as one mainstream of Christianity prays to its deceased who led holy lives, referring to them as "saints who have returned to their heavenly home," Hawaiians similarly pray to their ancestral spirits who have returned to their home. Depicting where this home is located, the Hawaiian traditionally has spoken of it as beyond the horizon and below these islands.

Further, attaching the color white to goodness and divinity, and black to the opposites, is a cultural phenomenon, nothing more. Different cultures have different preferences. One finds that holy men and women the world over speak interchangeably of the heights of prayer and the depths of prayer. They also speak of the blackness and the nothingness they experience in mystic union with the divine just as much as they speak of brightness.

It is a mistake to associate Hawaiian worship with evil or devil worship. Christian scriptures themselves say to test a spirit so that "by his works you will know him." Hawaiian gods are primarily a source of goodness, fruitfulness, and healing. And Hawaiians are no different from other peoples in praying to their gods for things that are good. It is true that sorcery has traditionally been practiced by some *kahunas*, but these people and their works have always been considered evil by the Hawaiian people, and they have never been a part of mainstream Hawaiian religious life and practice.

Pairing In The Universe

THE PRINCIPLE OF DUALISM, that things of the cosmos present themselves in paired opposites, was developed to a high degree by the Hawaiians. Applications are found in many areas of thought and practice. Because it demonstrates one of the basic laws by which the beings of the conscious universe were thought to interrelate and function, it is highly significant. Martha Beckwith, in her translation of the *Kumulipo*, makes the following comments about pairing:

> Another philosophic concept comes out in his [the Hawaiian's] way of accommodating himself as an individual to the physical universe in which he finds himself placed. He arrives at an organized conception of form through the pairing of opposites, one depending on the other to complete the whole. So ideas of night and day, light and darkness, male and female, land and water, rising and setting (of the sun), small and large, little and big, hard and light (of force), upright and prostrate (of position), upward and downward, toward and away (from the speaker), appear paired in repeated reiteration as a stylistic element in composition of chants, and function also in everyday language, where one pair lies implicit whenever its opposite is used in reference to the speaker.[1]

The Concept of Dualism in the Structural Format of the *Kumulipo*

Dualistic theory, that opposites are found paired throughout nature, is presented in several ways in the *Kumulipo*. It is obvious in the text material itself, and it is also found in the infra-structure of the chant. Chants often were built on an underlying structural format. And when several chants were combined, as seemingly happened with the *Kumulipo*, they were worked into an underlying infrastructure.

The grand theme of the *Kumulipo* is the detailing of evolutionary progression from the beginning, up the evolutionary ladder to man and the gods, and then up the genealogical lists to the life of an *ali'i nui*, Lono-i-ka-makahiki, who lived in the seventeenth century. This progress is told in a format of sixteen time periods or "*wā.*" Dualistic theory may first be observed in the division of these sixteen *wā* into two periods: the first seven *wā* take place in "Darkness" (*pō*), and the last nine take place in "Light" (*ao*).

Pō and *ao* are paired opposites in Hawaiian thought. The words often are translated as "darkness" and "light." But they may also be translated as "nothingness" in contrast to "existence"; as "the realm of the unknown in contrast to "the known"; or as "the period before arrival in these islands or before arrival in Polynesia" in contrast to "the 'modern' period." They may also be translated as "the realm of spirits," in contrast to "the realm of beings presently living." They are basic, paired divisions of reality.

Dualism in the Text of the *Kumulipo*

Throughout the chant, items are presented as paired opposites. Heaven and earth are the first paired beings that are met. Kumulipo (Source in deep blue black sea), a male, and Pō'ele (Black Pō), a female, are also mentioned, and it is through their interrelation that all begins. From them comes the coral polyp, followed by the higher species of plant and animal life—many of them presented in pairs—and eventually man. Two thousand generations of mankind are then given in genealogical lists which are arranged according to male-female paired opposites: the first born son, his wife; their first born son, his wife, etc.

In the "Refrain of Generation" which is repeated forty-four times during the first four wā of the chant, creatures developing in the sea are paired with those developing on land. To list a few:

> The *Akaha's* home was the sea
> Guarded by the *Ekahakaha* that grew in the forest.
> The *Akiaki* was born and lived in the sea
> Guarded by the *Manienie Akiaki* that grew in the forest
> The *Aalaula* was born and lived in the sea
> Guarded by the *Alaalawainui* that grew in the forest
> The *Manauea* was born and lived in the sea
> Guarded by the *Kalo Manauea* that grew in the forest.[2]

The words "guarded by" demonstrate the Hawaiian conviction that creatures of the land and the sea were actually paired by nature, and that some activity or responsibility attended this relationship.

Rubellite Kawena Johnson, discussing the *Kumulipo's* "Refrain of Generation" points out that among the species of nature which are paired, there are several paired opposites in the structure of the refrain itself. It reads in part:

> "Male for the narrow waters,
> Female for the broad waters.
> *Kane ia wai 'ololi*
> *'o ka wahine ia wai 'olola.*
>
> ...
> It is the god who enters,
> Not as a human does he enter.
> *'O ke akua ke komo*
> *'a'oe komo kanaka.*[3]

Not only are there contrasts of male with female and of gods with men which are obvious in the English, but, as Johnson notes, the Hawaiian words for the narrow waters and the broad waters, *'oloĪi* and *'oloĪā* are paired in their sounds. The high, tense, front vowel in *Īi* (narrow waters) is put in opposition to the open, relaxed vowel of *Īā*, (broad waters), she notes, thus pairing the contrast of sounds uttered by the human voice with the male-female antithesis which characterizes the two waters.[4]

It is interesting that much pairing in the *Kumulipo* is of things whose names share similar sounds. While it might be thought that pairing of species with similar sounding names in the chant was done only as a memory device, pairings of things with similar sounding names is also found in daily life. In Hawaiian plant medicine when one takes a dose of a special land-grown medicinal herb, the first food taken afterwards is the plant growing in the sea known to be paired with it, which shares a similar sounding name.[5] Physically putting together these edibles sharing same-sounding names was thought to effect the cure.

Gathering of plants for medicinal purposes was itself traditionally done in a ritual way: five were plucked with the left hand for Hina, balanced by five taken with the right hand for Kū.[6]

There were other pairings which involved Kū and Hina, the only divinities thought be "married." The name Kū meant "to stand upright"; Hina meant "to fall over from an upright position." The east was thought to be sacred to Kū, the west to Hina. Morning was sacred to Kū, afternoon to Hina. The rising sun was a felt presence of Kū, the setting sun of Hina. Houses and *heiaus* were frequently oriented with the doorway to the east to welcome the coming of Kū. The east gave direction to his presence; the west did the same for Hina.

Things Paired by Nature Function Together

Hawaiians thought that complementary relations existing between the rising and setting sun, and between east and west were of the same nature as the relation between the god Kū and the goddess Hina to whom these pairs were sacred. Things paired were like family—their "familial" relation determined that they would work to achieve common goals. Hawaiians did not look for an explanation for why things worked together. Why they did needed no more explanation than why relatives worked together.

Pairing of species was thought to be an innate characteristic of the species themselves. Their relation was inherent in them, not something decided from outside. It was thought that when one discovered what things were paired together, and discerned the purpose their pairing served, that insight could generally be brought to his service. Knowing how elements in nature worked together allowed man to work with nature to his greater benefit.

In summary, then, Hawaiians held it to be a principle that things of nature generally present themselves in paired opposites which function together to accomplish joint purposes.

We have now discussed the Hawaiians' view of the world's structure and how it developed; how they conceived of consciousness, and how they thought that the material universe was conscious and had from its earliest origins brought about its own development. We have also seen that, as it evolved, nature—existing as "thinking matter"—was indwelt by "thinking spirits," *akua*. Discussing the concept of *kino lau*, we noted that the great gods were thought to indwell much of nature, giving added dimensions of consciousness to the species they indwelt. We have seen that the things of nature, according to Hawaiian thought, are paired to function together for more successful accomplishment. And we have seen that through evolutionary descent and through descent from gods who have nature forms, man is related as kin to the conscious world of nature surrounding him.

The background knowledge spoken of in the Preface as necessary in order to understand the thought-framework from which Hawaiians approached their world is now in place. We can now explore the Hawaiian world-view itself, and see how man lives with nature in a conscious, interworking and interrelating community in which all beings have rights and obligations to one another, and all protect and care for one another.

Environmental Ethics
In Hawai'i

WHENEVER A GROUP OF PEOPLE live together in a community, eventually they formulate a body of rules to govern life in the community. Sometimes these are written down in a carefully worded form. They are then called "laws." At other times they are less formally specified. In this case they are called "moral codes" or "ethics."

Environmental ethics are concerned with more than just the human world and the rules through which humans living in a community interrelate peacefully with each other. Environmental ethics are concerned with the cosmic community. Environmental ethics are the various codes of rules which peoples of the world have developed so that they and the rest of the "environmental community" can live and progress together in harmony.

Different peoples treat the environment in ways consistent with their differing world-views. In the modern Western world-view, the environment is seen as material: it lacks any kind of awareness, and is there to be used at man's disposal. Western man in general treats the environment with little sensitivity because in his world-view it doesn't require sensitivity.

Strictly speaking, ethics are rules for communal living. And in order to have true "environmental ethics," individuals must recognize themselves as members of an interdependent community with other sentient "individuals of the environment": the soil, water, plants, and animals. Western man, in general, since he views the cosmos as insentient, does not accept that the environment can have an interdependent, fully "communal" relationship with him. For him, "community" can exist only among humans.

A stewardship model of environmental ethics has generally been espoused for Western culture: man is God's viceroy on earth, charged to govern wisely and preserve, not pillage and destroy, God's creation. However, this stewardship model has not strongly impressed Western patterns of action.

Our environment is fragile. In recent years there has been growing concern for its protection. Attempting to establish an intellectual basis for why man should take greater care for it, thinkers are turning to other cultures for alternative views and insights. Let us briefly touch on some of these views, considering their similarities and contrasts with Hawaiian environmental thought.

Chinese Taoism, with its emphasis on "flowing with nature" and living in harmony with nature, offers a good paradigm for environmental philosophy. In Taoist thought all things in nature come from the *Tao* and are of the same familial nature as the *Tao*. There is a familial "way" in which nature works or goes about doing what it does. To discover the *Tao*, or "the way" of nature, and to harmonize oneself with that flow brings personal happiness and cosmic harmony.

Taoism shares with Hawaiian thought a sense of communal family with the environment. But while the Taoist seeks to flow with nature and to harmonize himself with its way, the Hawaiian endeavors to bring nature into acting in a manner favorable to him. The Hawaiian knows he must extend himself for nature's benefit. He knows that it is his place to care for nature, not only by physical work, but also by spiritual activity. Nature, however, in turn has the obligation to respond—to provide for and to protect man.

In Taoist thought the king plays a pivotal role between nature and man. The ideal king is a sage who knows the way of nature and acts according to it in all of his actions. All of the people seek to follow the way of the sage king, and their actions thus flow along harmoniously with the *Tao*. When the king acts contrary to the *Tao*, all of nature falls out of harmony. Great storms arise and other calamities come upon the people. In Hawaiian thought the *ali'i nui* plays a somewhat similar role in that his chiefly presence of itself causes all of nature to work in harmony. His death or removal causes chaos throughout all of nature.

Also, although Taoism assumes that nature is aware of man and his actions, man has no need to communicate with it. Man's aims can be achieved by observing nature. The Hawaiian, however, communicates with nature in order to secure its cooperation.

The American Indians also approach the environment as sentient. The Ojibwa (Chippewa) Indians, for instance, think that the relationships among the animals in nature are social, and also that they reflect the structure of Ojibwa society. Animals are other-than-human persons, who have families, enjoy visiting, smoking, and so forth, just as the Ojibwas do. The correct (ethical) relationship of people to such other-than-human persons parallels the correct social manners of people with one another: gift-giving, entertaining, etc.

The Hawaiian also views the relationships among the things of nature as reflecting Hawaiian social structure. However, the Hawaiian's social structure is far more political and more hierarchical than the Ojibwa's who have no chiefs and practically no political structure at all. Hawaiians represent the natural order and the political order as one seamless, organic whole. The *Kumulipo* presents evolution as a hierarchy of beings with the land, sky, and sea, and the originative material from which they come at the base, then plants and animals in ascending order, and at the top, mankind. This hierarchical arrangement continues on in society, with outcasts at the bottom, then women, common men, various levels of chiefs and priests, and finally at the pinnacle, the *ali'i nui*. The Hawaiian believed that there must be order throughout this hierarchical structure if the whole of nature was to live and flourish. Removal of the *ali'i nui* would decapitate the whole order of nature. The land would die, and the people could not prosper.

In Hawaiian thought, with man at the top of the evolutionary ladder, all of nature was understood to serve man in the same way the commoner serves the chief. People might put up with a harsh and inconsiderate king throughout his life, but they could just as well overthrow him. People had rights to a good life lived in peace under a good chief. The environment served man in the same way that man served the chief. And the environment deserved respect, and the same caring and tending for that was found in human society. In Hawai'i, ideally the rights of all members of the cosmic community were recognized, and their needs dealt with. The Hawaiian sensed the response of the sentient world community around him and interrelated with it lovingly.

Expressions of Hawaiian Belief in a Conscious, Interrelating, Cosmic Community

Since sentience among all of the participants is such an important aspect of Hawaiian environmental ethics, let us look at a few more examples of how Hawaiians demonstrated their belief that the world around was conscious.

In the many prayers asking that life be given to the land, life was prayed to the land in the same way that it was prayed to the chief and the people, as this prayer from the *makahiki* ceremonies shows:

A season of plenty this.	*He kau ai keia.*
Earth yield thy plenty.	*E lu ka honua!*
This is a season of food.	*He kau ai keia.*
Life to the land!	*Ola ka aina!*
Life from Kane.	*Ola ia Kane,*
Kane the god of life.	*Kane ke akua ola.*
Life from Kanaloa!	*Ola ia Kanaloa!*
The wonder-working god.	*Ke akua kupueu.*
Life to the people!	*Ola na kanaka!*
Kane in the life-giving water, live!	*Kane i ka wai ola, e ola!*
Life to the king of the Makahiki!	*Ola ke alii Makahiki!*
Let it happen. The tapu is lifted.[1]	*Amama; ua noa.*

People interrelated with and depended on conscious nature in order to accomplish many tasks. A vivid example is found in the way the canoe-carving *kahuna* relied on the *'elepaio* bird to show him the qualities of the tree he had felled. "If the bird darted down and perched on the trunk of the tree and then ran along the trunk from one end to the other, [the *kahuna*] would know that it was perfect." If the opening was not to be carved on the side that was up, the bird would fly to a certain height and then circle over the tree, indicating that it should be turned. Where the bird would alight and sit for some time, the *kahuna* knew he would find some defect in the tree.[2]

At times nature assisted man in his efforts to foretell the success of an endeavor. For instance, in the month of June there were expeditions to fish for ʻōpelu. Before setting out, there were services in the *heiau*, followed by a meal. When the meal was completed,

> the priest commanded a man to go up the mountains to get *pala* fern, cautioning him that if he was caught in the rain to let him know. The man went up, found the *pala* fern, and while breaking it off, the rain fell. He came down feeling happy for being caught in the rain. When he had come into the presence of the priest, the latter asked him, "How fared you on your trip up?" He answered and said, "You told me to go up, and I have done so. My hands broke off the *pala* fern [and] the rain fell over me, and I was nearly bent with the cold." Then the priest said, "The omens are good. Tomorrow we will make a haul."[3]

How fully nature's mode of life was thought to parallel man's is exhibited in a passage written by Reverend William Ellis about an experience while travelling around the Big Island in 1827:

> We had not travelled far before we reached Ninole, a small village on the sea-shore, celebrated on account of a short pebbly beach called Koroa, the stones of which were reported to possess very singular properties: amongst others, that of propagating their species. The natives told us it was a *wahi pana* (place famous) for supplying the stones employed in making small adzes and hatchets, before they were acquainted with the use of iron; but

particularly for furnishing the stones of which the gods
were made, who presided over most of the games of
Hawaii. Some powers of discrimination, they told us,
were necessary to discover the stones which would
answer to being deified. When selected, they were taken
to the *heiau,* and there several ceremonies were performed
over them. Afterwards, when dressed, and taken to the
place where the games were practiced, if the parties to
whom they belonged were successful, their fame was
established; but if unsuccessful for several times together,
they were either broken to pieces, or thrown
contemptuously away. When any were removed for the
purpose of being transformed into gods, one of each sex
was generally selected; these were always wrapped very
carefully together in a piece of native cloth. After a
certain time, they said a small stone would be found with
them, which, when grown to the size of its parents, was
taken to the *heiau,* or temple, and afterwards made to
preside at the games.
We were really surprised at the tenacity with which this
last opinion was adhered to, not only by the poor people
of the place, but by several others, with whom we have
since conversed, and whom we should have supposed
better informed. It required all the argument and ridicule
that we could employ, to make them believe it could not
possibly be so.[4]

Examples of Man's Involvement
in Assisting Nature to Be Productive

Man was more than just an observer of the growth and
fertility of nature. At every level of society in pre-Cook
Hawai'i, examples are found of observances which either
limited man's freedom of action or required him to put forth
considerable effort in order to benefit nature. These
practices were undertaken as ethical obligations—man
doing his part in the communal relationship.

Besides laboring to cultivate his crops or to feed his
fishing grounds, man had a spiritual role in causing nature

to be productive. This activity could be as simple as prayer. Prayer, in ancient practice, was a deep, intense involvement with the deity. The Hawaiian prayed frequently. In every occupation there were private rituals which men performed. Kamakau, for instance, gives prayers the man said at every step of the cultivating process: prayers for cutting and hewing his digging stick, prayers for preparing the area for planting, prayers while doing the planting, prayers for rain to come upon his young slips, prayers for the young plants to bear fruit, prayers for the fruit to grow big and healthy, and, finally, prayers of thanksgiving performed at harvest.[5] Similar prayers and rituals were performed in other occupations.

Man's role in nurturing nature sometimes involved something much deeper than ordinary prayer—a spiritual or psychic extension beyond himself into unison with nature. This can be seen in rites which involve swallowing an eyeball of a fish. In the month of June, when the expeditions to fish for *'opelu* returned, a fish from the first haul was brought to the king. Fornander tells us, "The king then went to the shrine, where a priest prayed. They then prepared the king's fish, from which the king picked out the right eye and ate it."[6]

There is a well-known parallel to this in a *heiau* service during the *makahiki* ceremony, where the human impersonator of the god Kamohoali'i eats the eye of an *ulua* fish. In that case the god is said to take into his own being the eyeball of the fish, as a symbol of all *ulua* fish, with the purpose that all *ulua* might be nurtured and increased through the connection thus established with the nurturing god.[7] Most likely, when the chief ate of the eye of the *'opelu* from the first haul of the expedition, then, it was an act with the same purpose. The divine chief—who had a special chiefly nurturing relationship with all of nature—was establishing a connection between himself and the fish world, causing it to prosper and to become more prolific.

Another example of humans doing their part to benefit the environment is found in their ritual dancing in the *heiau*. Men participated in bringing about fertility in nature through such dancing. Handy writes,

> The erotic dancing of the tropical islands of Polynesia,
> which was in its origin a form of worship, was designed
> to stimulate and bring into action the mana of the gods
> who were believed to be animated by the same emotions
> as men, and on whose procreative activities the fecundity
> of human beings, the earth, and the sea depended.[8]

In the ritual the dancers called the gods within their bodies. They also, in their dancing, allowed themselves to move into a trance state. In the trance the barriers between them and surrounding nature came down. They experienced oneness with nature around them, allowing themselves to flow spiritually into nature, and nature to thoroughly permeate their being. Gods, men, and nature then being one, when the dancers performed the erotic actions of their fertility dance, the gods and nature—from which the dancers were at the time indistinguishable—would experience the desires and actions of the dancers. While joined with the gods and nature, the dancers' movements and gestures, along with their intent, effected the impregnation of nature by the divine.

Nature Cares for Man

In the cosmic community, when man did his part to assist nature in becoming fertile and productive, it became the ethical obligation of gods and nature to similarly care for man. Nature was believed to assist man in various ways. For example, Hawaiians used the *kī* (or *ti*) plant and its leaves as a protection from evil spirits. They planted it around their homes, wore leis and amulets made of *kī*, and used it to sprinkle salt water in the spirit-cleansing ritual which they called *pī* kai.[9] *Kī* was thought to prohibit spirits from causing harm to the person wearing it or otherwise putting themselves under its protection.

There were stones in the islands known for their curative powers. Such a stone lies on the beach at Pua'ena Point in the Waialua District of O'ahu.

> Hawaiians came to visit it from all over the island. Seaweed was placed on the stone and a petition for aid addressed to it before the injured part was touched to the stone. If the ceremony was properly performed, the cure would be certain to follow.[10]

There were also many stones that were thought to draw fish. Some were less than a foot long and carved in the shape of a fish. Called *Kū'ula* stones, they would draw fish to them as soon as they were put in the water.[11]

There were also certain rocks thought to have the power to grant women pregnancy. One such famous stone is *Ka-ule-o-Nānahoa* on the island of Moloka'i. Shaped like the male genitals, and being in size about 6'x12'x12', it was thought that if a woman climbed up and slept for the night in the cradle in the top of the penis, that she would become pregnant during her next sexual encounter.[12]

Some Items in the Hawaiian Code
of Environmental Ethics

The Hawaiian people, then, cared for nature. And nature cared for the people. But, were there specific sets of rules which humans observed in relation to the cosmic community? Environmental ethics in ancient Hawai'i were generally expressed in actions rather than dictums. Hawaiians observed general ethical practices but only rarely codified these into sets of ethical rules. However, one set of rules is recorded by Fornander, those that were observed by the family of a fisherman so that he would be successful in his fishing:[13]

It was customary with those whose vocation was that of fishing to have certain regulations. Before a person went out fishing, he would admonish those who remained at home not to do any act which would interfere with the fishing trip. He cautioned them in this wise:

1. The wife was forbidden from committing adultery.
2. Adultery by other inmates of the house of the fisherman was also forbidden.
3. Fighting was forbidden in the house of the person going out fishing.
4. Inquiries such as "Where is (the fisherman)" while he was out on the ocean were forbidden.
5. Eating the bait reserved by the fisherman was forbidden.
6. Covetousness during the fisherman's absence at sea was prohibited. If any one of these things was violated by those at home while one was out fishing his labor was in vain; by observing the sanctity of the house of those going out fishing, success would result.

The breaking of a hook was a recognized indication to the husband that his wife had committed adultery. The same would apply to all the inmates of the house.

Some people strictly observed these rules when a person went out fishing.

There are other *kapu*s regarding fishermen. Fishermen never wear red because the color is sacred to the god Kū who, in his form as Kū'ula, the god of fishing, would find it offensive. Further, fishermen never take bananas out in their boats because the banana is a *kino lau* of Kanaloa, the god of the ocean. In some areas just the opposite seems to be practiced as an alternative way of honoring these gods.

The most famous of the formal rules had to do with the *kapu*s surrounding eating. Some foods denied to women were forbidden because the foods were *kino lau* of the gods. For instance, women could not eat pig, because it was a *kino lau* of the god Lono as Kamapua'a; banana, because the banana tree was a form of the god Kāne; coconuts, because the coconut tree was a form of Kū; and sea turtle, sea tortoise, porpoise, whale, and the spotted sting ray, probably because they were all forms of Kanaloa.[14]

One rule still commonly observed is, "Never take anything without asking." To do so, even if it is a rock, is to invite upon one's self the displeasure of the spirits of the place or in the object. The way Hawaiians ask before picking a flower is a common example of the "asking rule."

It is also general practice to leave something as a replacement when something of value is taken. If one first asks and then leaves a proper offering, it is thought that he can usually feel free to remove what is desired.

One also learns to "Pick *'ohi'a* lehua blossoms only when one has returned all the way home from a trip to the mountains." To pick the flower sooner will cause it to rain.[15]

Another rule commonly observed today is "Don't take pork over the Pali (the cliff separating the Honolulu side of O'ahu from Kailua). One doing so might have his car stall and remain stalled until the pork is removed.[16] A reason sometimes given for this is that the area is sacred to Kamapua'a, the demigod who is half human half pig, and he causes the problem as a punishment for one's insensitivity.

Ghosts are a part of the cosmic community too. There are general rules about carrying food at night, especially pork, because of hungry ghosts. Tying the container with green *kī* (or *ti*) leaf or fresh bamboo or lele banana leaves commands ghosts to leave it and the carrier alone.[17]

Man's ethical practices in regard to nature may also be seen in the Hawaiian's treatment of *kalo* (or *taro*). Wakea was thought by the Hawaiians to have been their first human ancestor. According to tradition, his first-born child either was born prematurely and was malformed, or was born as a root. The child died. Wakea buried the first-born at the corner of his *hale* (house), and from it sprang the *kalo* (or *taro*) plant. He named it Haloa. When his second child was born, a human who would be the father of the Hawaiian people, he named him Haloa, also. The *kalo* plant, however, being the first-born, was genealogically superior to and more *kapu* than man himself, for man was the descendant of the second-born. *Kalo* has always been thought of by Hawaiians as being of a higher branch of cosmic lineage than man himself, and it has been given the deference and reverence of its place.[18] Even today among Hawaiian families, there might be much banter, joking, relating of ancecdotes, and matching wits while eating, but no unpleasant or malicious talk is allowed out of respect to the *poi* on the table which is the visible presence of Haloa,

the *kalo*.[19] If one should begin to "talk stink" about another,
the *poi* bowl is covered.[20]

Methods of Communicating with Nature

Early written records suggest that, rather than always
communicating directly with nature, Hawaiians frequently
prayed to gods to work with nature for them. Coming to
gods for this purpose, Hawaiians sometimes addressed
them in their high-god, spirit forms—their forms outside of
and beyond nature. A prayer addressed to gods in their
high-god forms reads:

> O Kane and Lono! Gods of the husbandmen,
> Give life to the land!
> Until the food...sprouts in the ground
> Until the leaves cover the land
> Great shall be your gift to us.
> O Kane and Lono.
> Let it happen. The tapu is lifted.[21]

At other times they prayed to gods in their nature *kino lau*.
A prayer where a specific god is addressed because help is
needed from a nature form he indwells is:

> O Lono of the broad leaf,
> Let the low-hanging cloud [a *kino lau* of Lono]
>   pour out its rain
> To make the crops flourish,
> Rain to make the *tapa* plant flourish.
> Wring out the dark rain clouds
> Of Lono in the heavens.[22]

There were also occasions when nature was addressed
directly. A direct prayer to nature by a successful fisherman
is recorded by Gutmanis:

> O the east, O the west   *E ka hikina, e ke komohana*
> O the north, O the south   *E ka akau, e ka hema,*

O above, O below, O the sun	E luna, e lalo, e ka la
Recognize me the fisherman	E ike ia'u i ka lawai'a
Look at the grumbling,	E nana i ka ohumu,
at the fruitfulness	i ka huahua
We are first; ours the last	He mua kaua, he hope ko kaua
Give me recognition, o rainy	E ike oe ia'u e ka la ua,
day, windy day, quiet day.	e ka la makani, e ka la malie
My day of course is that of	O ko'u la ho'i ia
the fisherman	ko ke kanaka lawai'a
Provided with line and hook	I lako i ke aho me ke makau
O sun, give me life	E ka la e. E ola ia'u
And to my wife, my children	I ka'u wahine, i ku'u keiki
and my parents.	i ko'u mau makua
Amama. The prayer kapu is	*Amama. Ua noa.*
lifted.[23]	

Relating another instance where nature is addressed directly, Handy and Handy write: "Surfers would whip the waves with *pōhuehue* vine and chant 'Arise, arise, ye great surfs from Kahiki, The powerful curling waves. Arise with the *pōhuehue*. Well up, long ranging surf.' The sea lashed with *pōhuehue* vines would become rough and dangerous "[24]

A prayer addressing nature directly which is said when a loved one sails away is given by Gutmanis:

O thou great ocean,	E ka moana nui
Thou deep seas	Kai hohonu
Let thy waves flow gently.	'E lana malie kou mau ale.
O thou strong winds blowing	'E ka makani nui ikaika,
Breathe softly and tenderly,	'E pa kolonahe, malie 'oe.
Go thou with serenity and peace,	'E nihi e ka hele
Let nothing bar your way.[25]	Mai ho'opa.

Communicating with gods rather than directly with nature frequently seems to have been preferred. The Hawaiian fisherman, for example, did not seem to have communicated with the fish, telling them to allow themselves to be caught. Possibly this was for efficiency. There was no need to communicate directly with the fish when the god of fishing had fully proven his effectiveness. It is also possible that it saved embarrassment. Unlike the Ojibwa Indians of America who believed that game animals freely gave themselves to the hunters if the hunters observed the correct behavior towards them, Hawaiians seem to have killed their prey thinking the animals as desirous of life as themselves. It was easier not to communicate with life forms one had to eat.

'Aloha 'Āina

Aldo Leopold, one of the first philosophers to work on environmental ethics, writes that "Ethics is beyond any even-exchange system of trade. It involves obligations to other community members over and above those dictated by self-interest." He argues that "no ethical relation...can exist without love, respect, and admiration."[26] Although this might be seen as adding unnecessary requisites for ethics, nevertheless love, respect, and admiration are fundamental to the Hawaiian philosophy of the environment. *Aloha 'āina*, love of the land, is an ancient concept which forms the basis for that philosophy. The phrase itself can be found in various ancient chants. In the Pele and Hiiaka Myth, Hiiaka chants to her beloved district, Puna—"*O Puna, 'āina aloha!*...O Puna, beloved land!"[27]

Hawaiian love for the land is further exemplified in the word, *kama-'āina* "child of the land." A person living in an area refers to himself as a *kama-'āina*, in contrast to a *malihini*, a "stranger."

The sayings and proverbs of the people also demonstrate their closeness to the land and their love for it. Mary

Kawena Pukui, who made a life-long study of the sayings and proverbs of the Hawaiians, stated that many sayings employ place names, which is "something completely lacking in Euro-American proverbial sayings."[28] The Hawaiian people so love the land, and live in such intimate harmony with it, that their proverbs cannot help but tell of that closeness and love.

Handy and Handy, in *Native Planters in Old Hawaii* also note that:

> a mystical or spiritual identification of the population with the land existed from very early times between the Hawaiian people— be they chiefs or commoners—and their homeland. This is abundantly exemplified in traditional mele (songs), in *pule* (prayer chants), and in genealogical records which associate the ancestors, primordial or more recent, with their individual homelands, celebrating always the outstanding qualities and features of those lands.[29]

Aloha 'āina was more than just a phrase, it was a way of life.

The Special Place of The Chief

We have seen that Hawaiians pictured their world as an ascending hierarchical whole with the levels of evolution reflecting and culminating in a stratified societal structure. Man stood at the apex of evolved nature. And at the pinnacle of human society—and therefore of all else—stood the *ali'i nui*. Usually translated as "high chief," from the time of Kamehameha I the *ali'i nui* was the king. Until Kamehameha I united the islands, each island usually had its own *ali'i nui*. And when districts of islands were ruled separately, each district was ruled by an *ali'i nui*.

Throughout Polynesia the *ali'i nui* was thought to have a special relationship with the land. In many island groups his relationship with the land was thought to cause crops to grow well and animals to proliferate.[1]

Many references to the chiefs' special relationship to the land can be found both in the works of the first generation of Hawaiian writers and in old chants and stories which have come down to us.

The chief regularly demonstrated his special place in relation to nature in *heiau* (temple) rituals. These rituals were conducted by priests, but they acted only in the place of, and for, the chief. At the conclusion of rituals, the chief made the services his, and effected what the rituals had intended, by saying *'āmama*, which meant "Let it happen." It was believed that the chief had the power to effect then and there the changes in nature which had been sought, and that he did this with the command, *'Āmama*, "Let it happen."[2]

Another ritual following from the chief's special relationship with nature is found in the *makahiki* ceremony. The *makahiki* is at basis a seasonal fertility rite honoring the god of agriculture, Lono. It is thought to have developed from an ancient story motif from which also came the Orpheus and Eurydice, Demeter and Persephone, Isanagi and Isanami, and other tales which depict the necessary death of nature in the autumn so that it might be reborn anew in the spring.[3] In the *makahiki* rite, the high chief and the fertility god, Lono, seem either to trade places or to blend into one another. When the god is brought into the presence of the chief, Malo says that the chief is "sitting in the mystic rite of Lono, *e noho ana ke alii nui i ka Iui o Lono*."[4] The king puts a *lei niho palaoa*, the *lei* worn only by chiefs, around the neck of the god. The god then proceeds around the island for a month receiving tribute and taxes—a task which would seem more proper for the chief than the god—while the chief stays in the temple (*heiau*).[5] When the great procession returns from its tribute-collecting trip around the island, the chief does not go directly to greet it. Rather, he gets into a canoe and sails out into sea. Then he returns, portraying the formal, yearly return of the god Lono. When he steps out of the canoe, he is met by men throwing spears which he must dodge in order to prove his divinity. If he survives this, a single spear is then touched to his breast in a symbolic killing of Lono, the god of nature.[6] The king then seems to reassume his role as king.[7] The tribute is divided up. A portion is given for the god, Lono; the high chief keeps a portion; and the rest is divided among the lesser chiefs. A canoe which has been carved for Lono is then laden with his portion, carried to the sea, and led out to catch the current in order to sail back to Kahiki. Lono is thought to sail with the canoe; the long *makahiki* ceremony is over; and the chief resumes his normal role.

The numerous Hawaiian chants honoring the genitals of the chiefs further demonstrate the role of the chief in the fertility of nature. Called *mele ma'i*, with hearty sexual humor they tell of the genitals (*ma'i*) of the chief and of the pleasures of coition he enjoys. Often the double-meaning words chosen to symbolize the chief's *ma'i* (genitals) and their activity suggest the connection of the fertility of the chief with the fertility of nature. For example, his penis might be referred to as a tree or a branch, his testicles as leaves. Or his penis might be the *lei* needle threading a flower *lei*. While one purpose of the chant is to honor his *ma'i* which will produce future *ali'i* to lead the people, his penis is also seen as the symbol of fertility for the land, since he is the instrument through which that fertility will come.[8] *Mele ma'i* for *ali'i* are part of every traditional *hula* performance.

Hawaiian *ali'i* were convinced they had a special control over nature, and they were willing to demonstrate that they did. Even in post-Cook times, there are reports of *ali'i* halting lava flows. Kamehameha I is said to have saved his fishponds from approaching lava by standing before the flow, making offerings, and appeasing the goddess Pele.[9]

Newspaper accounts and letters of missionaries who witnessed a similar event in 1881 tell how Princess Ruth, who rejected the Christian religion of the *haole* (white man or foreigner), demonstrated the power of both her station and of the old religion by standing before a lava flow at the outskirts of Hilo, making offerings to that presence of Pele, and stopping the flow before her.[10]

In Hawaiian thought, the king controls nature and nourishes and sustains it by his presence alone. He maintains order in nature just as he maintains it in human society. So close is his relation with the lands that when he dies, the lands die.

This is seen in the chant "Fallen is the Chief," a prophecy uttered by Keaulumoku eight years before the conquest of the Big Island by Kamehameha I, foretelling that conquest.[11] In the chant Keaulumoku prophesied the death of the chief, Keoua, and described also the death of his lands—Hilo, Puna, and Kā'u—which would follow the death of their chief.

The spirit of the land has fled;	*Ua lele ka hoaka o ka aina*
The soul of the land is flown upward	*Ka uhane o ka moku eia iluna*
The pebbles of Palila have appeared,	*Ua ikea na iliili a Palila*
The glory of the land is thrown into a place of death.	*Ua hoolei ia i kahi make,*
Ka'u is dead.	*Kau make la.*
Ka'u is slain by these conquerers	*Make Kau e lakou nei,*
Now the soul staggers	*Ke newa mai nei ka uhane*
The *'uhane kinowailua* (soul) of the land	*Ka uhane kinowailua o ka aina*
The *kinowailua* (souls) of the three districts:	*Ke kinowailua o na kolu,*
Ka'u, Puna, and Hilo[12]	*O Kau, o Puna, o Hilo.*

Later,[13] still speaking of the lands, he says those important words,

Puna is dead! Puna is dead!...	*Make Puna e! Make Puna!*
The breath of life (*ea*) and	*Ua lilo ke ea,*
the breathing are gone,	*me ka hanu,*
the spirit has fled.	*ua haalele loa ke aho.*

The soul of the land, and "its living breath" (*ke ea o ka ʻāina*), leave it just as the chief's soul and his living breath (*ea*) leave his body.

Because man stands at the pinnacle of evolution and because the *aliʻi nui* stands at the head of human society, when the chief is in his place, all of nature works together. His presence holds everything together. When he dies, everything comes apart, including the societal structure. People go about nude and engage in sexual acts in public. They gash themselves, knock out their teeth, shave their heads, and burn marks on their bodies to remember the chief. The *kapu* system also comes apart, completing the disorder throughout all of nature. Women are allowed to enter the *heiau*, to eat bananas, coconuts, and pork, and to climb over the sacred places. And women and men eat together.[14]

It then devolves upon the new *aliʻi nui* to give new life to the land and to restore order to nature. After the mourning period, when the new *aliʻi nui* is enthroned, he restores the direction and structure of society, reestablishing order among the people by reinstating the *kapu* system. Through his presence and his prayers, he then builds a new relationship with the gods and with nature, revivifying nature and setting everything right again. The chant "Fallen Is The Chief" tells of a new chief as he takes over the land.

The island also was untamed, that the chief knew well.
On his becoming guardian it was more and more tamed.
It was caught with a rope,
    the voice soothing the island was a net.
It was well-fed with the bait,
    it was choked with the cuttlefish.
He fed the small fish,
    he gathered them together like bonito.
He filled their open mouths with the bait.
Streams of country people of the island follow;
Here the red tail of the land sweeps around
Like a well fed favorite dog.[15]

Once the new chief reestablished the *kapu* system and brought order back to society, and once he calmed nature and brought it under his nurturing control, then it once more could be said, *Ua mau ke ea o ka ʻāina* (The living breath of the land continues on) *i ka pono* (since [the king is in his place of leadership and] everything is ordered correctly again).

The True Meaning Of The State Motto Of Hawai'i

ALTHOUGH THE HAWAIIAN WORLD-VIEW is in so many aspects directly contraposed to the Western view, today most Western-thinking residents of Hawai'i are not even aware that there is a native Hawaiian world-view which differs from their own. One of the reasons for this is that the words Hawaiians use to express their ideas are spoken from the context and meaning of one world-view, but they are given a different meaning by the hearer because they are comprehended in the context of his differing world-view.

A long-standing example of this can be found with the state motto, *Ua mau ke ea o ka ʻāina i ka pono.* Today, this is officially translated, "The life of the land is perpetuated in righteousness." Most readers of this sentence in English take it as straightforward prose. Few reflect on it sufficiently to realize that, taken literally, the motto doesn't make any sense to a Western-thinking person: "The life of the land is perpetuated in righteousness." In grasping for meaning, Westerners most frequently focus on the word "righteousness" as the word upon which to base their interpretation. They understand the motto to mean something like, "The state runs well when the politicians and/or the people live righteously."[1]

Such an unfounded rendering has plagued the motto since the beginning. The first published discussion about the saying appeared in the May 31, 1845, edition of *The Polynesian*, less than two years after its utterance, in an unsigned article attributed to Robert C. Wyllie, Foreign Minister in the government of Kamehameha III. Focusing on "righteousness," he wrote:

> The motto is, Ua mau ke ea o ka aina i ka pono, the life of the land is preserved by righteousness. It refers to the speech of the king at the time of cession, February 25, 1843. 'I have given away the life of the land. I have hope that the life of the land will be restored when my conduct is justified.' It very naturally alludes to the righteousness of the British Government, in returning the Islands to their legal sovereign, to the righteousness of the Hawaiians which secured restoration, and to the general principle, that it is only by righteousness that national existance (sic) is preserved.[2]

Mottos frequently exhort the populace to pursue high principles and ideals, so Wyllie's seizing upon the idea of "righteousness" was to be expected. It fit in with his European expectations. But after choosing "righteousness" as his central concept, he became confused about what Kamehameha III wished to credit with "righteousness." Thus he named three possible areas of righteous practice to cover all of the likely instances.

While there is little question that this saying had more than one meaning, since multiple, even hidden, meanings (*kaona*) were the mark of good Hawaiian rhetoric, the meanings which Wyllie offered are probably not very close to what the king intended. To a native Hawaiian listener, the king's Hawaiian words, "*i ka pono,*" did not mean "in righteousness." They meant, rather, "when things are properly ordered" or "when things are as they should be."

How could Wyllie have misinterpreted the words? Even though he was one of the three *haoles* (white men) in the Privy Council of the king and was unquestionably one of the most important people in the government, Wyllie had not even arrived in the islands until the year after the takeover and restoration had taken place,[3] and he had lived in Hawai'i for only one year when he wrote his article. More importantly, he neither spoke nor understood the Hawaiian language.[4] It is thus most unlikely that he understood the world-view from which the words were spoken. Yet his interpretation, unfortunately, has become the basis for all later discussion of the motto.

The incident which led to the utterance of the famous words began when the British consul laid claim to property purportedly deeded to him by two second-ranking chiefs. This claim was not recognized by the king. The whole affair took place before the division of lands among chiefs and commoners, at a time when the king still owned all the property in the islands. The king regularly awarded lands to chiefs, but they held them at his pleasure during their lives, and all lands reverted back to the king when the awardee died. Any gift or sale by lower chiefs, therefore, was of lands not theirs to give.

At the request of the British consul who was asserting the land title, Lord George Paulet was sent with the battleship *Carysfort* to protect "British interests" in the islands. With the *Carysfort* to back them up, Britishers began making exorbitant claims and extorting all kinds of concessions from the kingdom. It became obvious that Paulet was aiming at annexation of the islands. Threatened with use of British force and having no viable alternative, after weeks of pressure, Kamehameha III, having followed in all of his actions what he and his advisors thought would later be affirmed as the proper procedures, eventually ceded the islands to Britain. The cession was to be temporary. In the meantime, every effort would be made to win back sovereignty. Emissaries would be sent to England with the facts, asking that Kamehameha III's original stand in regard to the lands be recognized as lawful.

At the time he ceded the kingdom to the British, knowing his relationship with the land and how the land was conscious of his leadership and nurtured by his rule, and knowing that the lands would die when their *ali'i* was taken from them, the king came before the people and pronounced, "Listen to me, all of you. I tell you, I am troubled. [But] the trouble I am being caused has no grounds in law, and since this is true, I have given away the life of our land (*ke ea o ka 'āina*). You have heard it. But my being *ali'i* over you and your well-being will continue, because I have hope that the life of the land (*ke ea o ka 'āina*) will be returned when my past actions are recognized as lawful."[5]

The concern of Kamehameha III in speaking these words was for "*ke ea o ka 'āina*" and its continuance. *Ke ea o ka 'āina* may be translated "the life of the land," but in Hawaiian *ea* means more than just "life." It means "the living breath." And even more specifically, it means the "life-force" which manifests itself as breath in man, and which also exists in everything in the cosmos. For most ancient peoples, the living breath was the sign of the life-force in a person. When one stopped breathing, the life-force had gone.

In the evolutionary thought found in several island groups of Polynesia, this "life-force" is mentioned as something possessed by all of nature. In the chant of the New Zealand Maoris discussed in chapter five, the "living breath" or the "life force," comes into the evolutionary scheme after the emergence of thought, remembrance, mind, desire, and word, but before the emergence of any material being. The chant reads, "The Third Period...From the nothing the increase...the abundance...the power of increasing, **the living breath**. It dwelt in empty space, It produced the atmosphere which is above us."

The people of Mangaia in the Cook Islands who depicted the world as a coconut (in the drawing shown in chapter three of this book) also placed "Breathing or Life" early in the process of creation, making it a characteristic common to all of nature.[6]

Kamehameha III, in speaking about *ke ea o ka 'aina*, was referring to that same "living breath" or "life force." He knew it to be the basis of life in all of surrounding nature. As he ceded rule of the lands to Britain, he knew that his action would cause a rupture in his chiefly, nurturing rapport with the lands. The lands themselves would suffer during this time of cession and could die. But he had hopes that once the lands were returned, he could again bring them under his chiefly nurturing power, and once all things were again *pono*, the lands would flourish as they had.

Five months later, on July 31, 1843, the lands were restored by Admiral Thomas. At that time the king came before the people again on the steps of Kawaiaha'o Church and proclaimed, "*Ua mau ka ea o ka 'aina i ka pono.*" Two meanings were understood by his Hawaiian listeners. Referring to the correctness of the king's own actions which led up to the takeover, one meaning was, "The life of the land continues since the actions taken were proper." But the more important meaning for the Hawaiians was that the king had reestablished his relationship with the land. The words meant, "The life of the land goes on, now that things are as they should be again," or "The life of the land continues, now that things are properly ordered," or "The life force continues in nature; nature lives on and prospers, now that the king has been restored to his proper place and has resumed his nurturing relationship with it."[7]

Conclusion

Today the lands are again suffering. Raped, plundered, gouged, covered over with cities of concrete by non-Hawaiians whose only concern is to amass personal fortunes, the lands wane.

New people in these islands approach them with the Western mind frame. For them, the lands are part of the material realm—they lack any kind of life or awareness and exist only to be used, placed completely at man's disposal. A common attitude is, "Leave enough of nature showing to still draw tourists, but cover the rest over with something that will make money."

Unaware of the long-established relationship of man with the land, and uncaring that surrounding nature when loved and cared for will love and care for in return, modern Americans are concerned to make Hawai'i the economic center of the Pacific: the wealth and power now slipping away from Hong Kong is sought for these islands. Massive tracts of land are being sold for Japanese developments, sometimes to be used exclusively by foreigners. No part of our islands is safe from development; all is prey for speculators. But what is all this bringing us?

Is it bringing us prosperity?   It brings a few jobs, but studies show that construction projects always bring in large numbers of immigrant workers from continental America or Asia.   These newcomers add to the traffic, add to school overcrowding, and increase pressure on the fragile water supply.   The new people also need homes.   They compete with the people of the area for the few houses available. Rents are bid up, doubling and tripling.   Outsiders frequently are able to pay the higher prices.   When there are just so many homes available, and when all of the homes have been priced beyond their reach, local people at the bottom of the economic spectrum are forced to move onto the beaches.   The problem gets worse with every new wave of immigrants, for the newcomers add to the numbers of Hawaiian residents with Western expectations and "developmental" values.   Where is the **good** in all of this for **our** people?

Will "development" bring us happiness?   Who is really happy in the world?   Is it the high-powered, fast-paced individualist who spends every resource of time, energy, and thought building and maintaining a financial empire? Is it those who have embraced the consumer mentality, believing that more possessions bring more happiness?

Is it not possible that Hawaiians and their world-view have something of eminent value to offer people of the modern world?   When the followers of Descartes began to teach that the surrounding environment was only insentient, mechanical matter, they cut man off from communication with the greatest part of his universe.   They alienated him from the community of nature in which he had always been a participant.   They took from him his fundamental sense of belonging, his feeling of being "at home" in the world.   They severed him from his most fundamental roots. Ever since, Western man has been plagued with feelings of dissatisfaction and lack of "wholeness." He wanders from project to project searching for fulfillment.

The Hawaiian world view has that grounding in reality that gives people fulfillment, contentment, and "at homeness" with oneself in the world. While viewing themselves as the highest evolutionary development, Hawaiians also see themselves as the continuation of cognizant nature, rather than as the **only** beings that think. Descended from and related as family to the sentient world about them, Hawaiians participate in a world not made up of cold, inert objects, but rather of warm, conscious beings, many of whom can be called upon for assistance, guidance, and reassurance. Hawaiians know how they fit into the world. In touch with the land, the sky, and the sea, they have the fulfillment and sense of belongingness for which Westerners search.

Those bent on developing these islands have nothing to offer the Hawaiian but their problems and their alienation from nature.

The preamble to the Constitution of the State of Hawai'i begins as follows:

> We, the people of Hawai'i, grateful for Divine Guidance, and mindful of our Hawaiian heritage and uniqueness as an island State, dedicate our efforts to fulfill the philosophy decreed by the Hawai'i State Motto, "*Ua mau ke ea o ka 'aina i ka pono.*"

The framers of this preamble, who so carefully hammered out these words, were obviously inspired to write what they did. All of conscious nature, perhaps, was aware of their work and guiding their hands as, perhaps without their knowing it, they committed the people of the state to fulfill the philosophy of the State motto. For the philosophy behind *Ua mau ke ea o ka 'āina i ka pono* is that the lands will be brought to life again only when all things are again *pono*. And *pono* requires that a native Hawaiian be restored as *ali'i nui* and that he begin exercising his chiefly rule over, and nurturing rapport with, the lands.

Where is that native Hawaiian *ali'i nui* who will reassert control? Control over the people, control over their developmental drives and their money-lust, and control over escalating growth? Where is the *ali'i nui* who will reassert loving, nourishing control over the lands and assure their proper development?

The preamble continues:

> We reserve the right to control our destiny, to nurture the integrity of our people and culture, and to preserve the quality of life that we desire.

Unless there is a complete turn in the direction set over the last century, there is little hope for the preservation of either the Hawaiian way of life or the Hawaiian people. Both continue to be pushed further aside.

The winds of change are blowing, however. Talk of sovereignty is in the air. The Hawaiian people seek the return of lands which will be inalienably theirs—territory belonging to a native Hawaiian nation. Among the lands sought are large areas on each island where man and the lands still live together in harmony and community. With the return of lands to Hawaiian control, Hawaiians can once again rebuild their society. They can reestablish their relationship with the land, and they can renew their community with conscious surrounding nature.

Then, when the chief is in his place, and nature and society are functioning together in harmony, it can truly be said again, *Ua mau ke ea o ka ʻāina i ka pono* — The life of the land continues now that all has been set right again.

ENDNOTES

Passing On Knowledge In Ancient Hawai'i

1 Translation by author of the original text found in *Kepelino's Traditions of Hawai'i* tr. by Martha Warren Beckwith, 1932. rpt. Millwood: Kraus 1978. pp. 131-2.

> *Ke Kakaolelo, oia no ka mea, a mau mea paha, e loio ana i*
> *ke ano o kela keia mooolelo kahiko, a e hooponopono ana i*
> *na mea a lakou e hooholo ai, a e olepu ana i na mea*
> *kupono ole o kela keia mooolelo o ia kau aku ia kau aku.*
> *A o ia poe, ua mau lakou ma ko lakou oihana iho; a ua*
> *lilo ia welo, he welo Kakaolelo.*

2 David Malo, *Hawaiian Antiquities: Moolelo Hawai'i*. Translated by Nathaniel B. Emerson. 1898. rpt. Honolulu: Bishop Museum Press, 1971, in a footnote by Emerson, p. 140. Some Hawaiian words were deleted from this quotation by the author in order to make it read more smoothly.

Samuel Kamakau in *Ruling Chiefs of Hawai'i* also speaks of a "house of instruction." He calls it an *oahualua*. p. 238.

3 Abraham Fornander, *An Account of the Polynesian Race: Its Origin and Migrations*. Vols. I-III. 1878, 1880, 1885. rpt. Rutland: Tuttle, 1969, p. 279.

The Hawaiian View Of The Universe

1 The entire cosmic structure presented here comes from David Malo, *Hawaiian Antiquities Moolelo Hawai'i*. Translated by Nathaniel B. Emerson. 1898. rpt. Honolulu: Bishop Museum Press, 1971, Chapter 6, pp. 12-6.

2 Malo, *Hawaiian Antiquities*, p. 26, Section 6.

3 This can be seen in the stories of fishing up the islands, in references to the islands as fish (See *Kumulipo*, *wa* #15 where the great fish, Pimoe, is synonymous with Kaua'i. Also Mary Kawena Pukui and Samuel Elbert, Hawaiian Dictionary, Honolulu: University of Hawai'i Press, 1971, p. 396), and in the story of Maui attempting to bring the islands together. See Martha Warren Beckwith, *Hawaiian Mythology*, Honolulu: University of Hawai'i Press, 1970 pp.227-37.

4 Martha Beckwith, *The Kumulipo*. Honolulu: University of Hawai'i Press, 1972. p. 44. She says that *walewale* has the sense of a thick glutinous

substance associated with birth: it is the afterbirth of humans and animals; it is also the slime in which coral polyps are born; and it is the slimy silt on the bottom of the sea.

5   Peter H. Buck, *Vikings of the Pacific*, Chicago: University of Chicago Press, 1938, p. 247.

6   Among others, see Beckwith, *Hawaiian Mythology*, p. 227, and Buck, *Vikings of the Pacific*, p. 55.   Elsewhere Tangaloa is also credited with fishing up Tonga. (Teuira Henry, *Ancient Tahiti*, Bernice Pauahi Bishop Museum, Bulletin No. 48. 1928 rpt. New York: Kraus, 1971, p. 346.)

7   Beckwith, *Kumulipo* p. 163. Punctuation in the quotation altered by this author.

8   Nathaniel B. Emerson, ftnt. in Malo, *Hawaiian Antiquities*, p. 15.

9   William Wyatt Gill, *Myths and Songs from the South Pacific*, New York: Arno Press, 1977, pp.1-5.

10   Gill, *Myths and Songs, Era, e te matakeinanga, no roro i Te-papa- rairai i Vatea.* p. 7.

11   J. Frank Stimson, *Tuamotuan Religion*, Bernice Pauahi Bishop Museum, Bulletin No. 103. 1933 rpt. New York: Kraus, 1971, p. 63.

12   Malo, *Hawaiian Antiquities*, p. 9.

13   Malo, *Hawaiian Antiquities*, pp. 7-8.

14   Because the tradewinds hit the Marquesas and Tahiti from the east, just as they do in Hawai'i, all of these islands are said to face the same direction.   Thus the front of their islands faces the back of the Hawaiian chain.
It might also be noted here that Tua-motu means "island back." The Tuamotus were so named by the Tahitians because they lay beyond the back or to the back of the Tahitian islands.

15   William Ellis, *Polynesian Researches, Hawai'i*, pp. 250-1.

16   Fornander, *Account*, I, pp.25, 26, 31, passim.

17   David Malo for instance, notes that north is spoken of as *luna* or *i luna* (above), and south is spoken of as *lalo* or down. (Malo, *Hawaiian Antiquities*, p. 9.)   Fornander states that *lepo*, which ordinarily means "ground" or "dirt" or "earth," also means "south." (Fornander, *Account*, I, p. 17.)
It would be interesting to go back now and re-study the original Hawiian version of all stories dealing with *po*. It might be that the round-world view which was held by the early translators—with hell in the underground underworld—is actually responsible for more of the idea that po is beneath us than was actually merited by the writings. Yet it must also be recognized that it was strong Hawaiian and Polynesian

tradition that one of the ways souls could reach p̄o was to descend through the roots of a certain tree.

18 J. Frank Stimson, Tuamotuan Religion, pp. 63 and 64.

19 William Wyatt Gill, *Myths and Songs*, pp 1-5.

20 Beckwith, *Hawaiian Mythology*, p. 50, states that Kahoali'i lives where the sun and the moon travel under the earth. I have presumed that the sun and the moon travel through the lowest level of the cosmos, since they travel against ka lani pa'a, the outermost level of the sky. Beckwith also says that Kumuhonua is Kahoali'i.

21 E.S. Craighill Handy and Elizabeth Green Handy, *Native Planters in Old Hawai'i*, Bernice P. Bishop Museum Bulletin No. 233. Honolulu: Bishop Museum Press, 1978, p.43. "Kumuhonua...was...in one genealogy...mated to Lalohonua [Earth bottom or earth depth] He cites Abraham Fornander, *Fornander Collection of Hawaiian Antiquities and Folklore*, Edited by Thomas G. Thrum, *Memoirs of the Bernice Pauahi Bishop Museum*, No. VI. 1917, rpt. Millwood: Kraus, 1974, p. 269.

22 David Malo, *Hawaiian Antiquities*, p. 3.

23 David Malo, *Hawaiian Antiquities*, 1903, p. 21; 1951, p. 3. Another mention of the taproot of the earth is found in a chant by Liholiho (King Kamehameha II) referred to by John Charlot, p. 111 of his book, *Chanting the Universe*, Hong Kong: Emphasis International, 1983.

Spirit And Matter In Hawaiian Thought

1 *Akua*, spirit consciousness, is used synonymously with '*uhane* or soul. It may also be used interchangably with *aka*. *Kepelino's Traditions*, on pp. 54-5, equates *akua* with man's soul, the '*uhane*. And '*uhane* is used interchangeably with *aka* "reflection" (E.g. *Fornander Collection*, VI, p. 452.). It is also used interchangeably with *kino wailua* or *aka kino wailua*, the soul that leaves the body at death. (See Fornander, *ibid.*, p.370.) For *akua* as synonymous with essence, the next footnote will show that gods ate the essences of things. William Ellis talking with residents of the Big Island in 1923, was told that "all of the souls of the departed went to the p̄o, place of night, and were annihilated, or eaten by the gods there." [William Ellis, Polynesian Researches: Hawai'i. Vol. IV. 1842. rpt. Rutland: Tuttle, 1969. p. 366] Gods eat souls of men; gods eat only essences; therefore the souls of men are essences. The souls of men are *akua*; therefore, *akua* are essences.

It might be noted here that Lorrin Andrews, *A Dictionary of the Hawaiian Language*, 1865. rpt. Rutland: Tuttle, 1974, p. 536, gives *he mea kino* as a translation for "matter."

2   June Gutmanis, *Na Pule Kahiko: Ancient Hawaiian Prayers.* Honolulu: Editions Limited, 1983, p. 81.

3 This short prayer is given in the Pukui-Elbert *Hawaiian Dictionary,* under *aka.*

4 Lorrin Andrews, *A Dictionary of the Hawaiian Language,* 1865. rpt. Rutland: Tuttle, 1974, p.44, under entry for *akua.*

5 Kepelino, *Kepelino's Traditions,* pp. 54-5.

6 Kepelino, *Kepelino's Traditions,* pp. 54-5.

7 Samuel M. Kamakau, *Ke Au 'Oko'a,* October 13, 1870, and October 20, 1870. June Gutmanis, *Na Pule Kahiko,* p. 46. For thorough treatment see the section *"Kino Akua*: The Higher *Akua* or *'Aumakua* Aspects of the Self,"* in the chapter on the *"Self"* in *A Philosophical Analysis of Pre-European Contact Hawaiian Thought,* by the present author.

8 Abraham Fornander, *Fornander Collection,* No. IV.   pp. 566. Kaulanapokii, was "a woman who had supernatural powers (*He wahine mana*) and could see things." She had the power to see her brother who had been killed, and the power (*ka mana*) to prematurely bring on labor pains in her sister.

9 Mary Kawena Pukui, E.W. Haertig, and Catherine A. Lee, *Nana I Ke Kumu,* Volume I, Honolulu: Queen Liliuokalani's Childrens Center Press, 1972, p. 80.

10 Kamapua'a, for instance, speaks directly to his material bodies. See Kahiolo, G.W. *He Moolelo No Kamapuaa.* Translated by Esther T. Mookini, Erin C. Neizmen, and David Tom. Honolulu: Hawaiian Studies Program, University of Hawai'i., 1978, pp. 69, 70, 45, 85, and compare with p. 181.

11 "Kalanimanuia." *Fornander Collection* Vol. IV p. 551-2. It might be argued that the parts of the body which returned were not the parts, exactly, but rather their beauty. However, the whole story in the original language supports the idea that it is the body parts themselves that are spoken of.

12 Cf. *Fornander Collection,* Vol. VI, p. 144.

Evolutionary Theory In Polynesia

1   Rubellite Kawena Johnson, *Kumulipo: Hawaiian Chant of Creation.* Vol. I Honolulu: Topgallant, 1981, pp.86-7.

2   Robert Wood Williamson, *Religious and Cosmic Beliefs of Central Polynesia,* Vol. I, London: Cambridge University, 1933, pp. 3-8.

3 According to the currently accepted settlement pattern for Polynesia, Tonga was the first island group settled, then Samoa, and then the Marquesas far to the east. From the Marquesas, the Polynesians advanced south-east to Easter Island, north to Hawai'i, and southwest to Tahiti (the Society Islands). The Society Islands are thought to be the spawning place for a high, eastern Polynesian culture. When this cultural advance was well along the way, New Zealand was settled by these people. Later, the Society Islanders reestablished contact with and sent groups of emigres to the Hawaiian Islands. Since evolutionary theory is found in both Hawai'i and New Zealand, and since these two peoples have no accepted history of contact with each other after the Tahitian migration to Hawai'i, the basic concept of evolution must have been common to Polynesian thought at least before these people left the Society Islands.

4 Williamson, *Religious and Cosmic Beliefs*, p. 4.

5 Williamson cites George Turner, *Nineteen Years In Polynesia*, London, 1861, Pg. 6, sq.

6 *Life On Earth* was a thirteen week series on evolution, supervised and produced by David Attenborough, and shown on Public Television in 1983 and 1984. See particularly weeks one through three. Copies of the entire series are available at Sinclair Library on the University of Hawai'i Manoa campus.

7 This chant is found in Richard Taylor, *Te Ika a Maui or New Zealand and Its Inhabitants*. London, 1870, pp. 109-10. It is discussed and amplified by Paul Radin, *Primitive Man as Philosopher*, New York: Dover, 1957, pp. 293-5.

8 Rubellite Kawena Johnson, *Kumulipo*, p. 45.

9 Rubellite Kawena Johnson, *Kumulipo*, pp. 4 - 5

10 It is possible to read the *Kumulipo* as stating that the coral evolved through from the *walewale*, the slimy silt-covered seabed which also gave birth to the lands, making the *walewale* an intermediary step in the evolution from *po*. Such an interpretation is consistent with stories of Maui fishing up the islands, and of Kapu-he'e-ua-nui fishing up coral pieces which were transformed into islands.

11 Malo, *Hawaiian Antiquities*, p. 3.

12 Martha Beckwith, *Kumulipo*, p. 58. Emphasis by present author.

13 Martha Beckwith, *Kumulipo*, p. 187.
Hanau ka (name) noho i kai
Kia'i ia e ka (name) noho i uka
He pou he'e i ka wawa
He nuku, he wai ka 'ai a ka la'au

O ke akua ke komo, 'a'oe komo kanaka.
"Hanau kane ia wai'ololi, o ka wahine ia wai'olola.

14   This is supported by Beckwith, *Kumulipo*, p.54.

15   Michael Kioni Dudley, *A Philosophical Analysis of Pre-European-Contact Hawaiian Thought*, dissertation available at Hamilton Library, University of Hawai'i, 1986. See Chapter 7.

16   The Maori chants cited above have consciousness pre-existent to any kind of material being. Chants from other archipelagoes frequently have gods pre-existing matter. Existence of this kind of thought elsewhere gives an indication of what might have existed in Hawai'i, but it does not establish the case. For examples, see Robert Wood Williamson, *Religious and Cosmic Beliefs of Central Polynesia*, Vol. I, London: Cambridge University, 1933, pp. 1-16.

17   Belief in kinship with animals is most likely ancient, pre-dating the entry of the people into Polynesia. In Melanesia the same animals which the Hawaiians think themselves to be descended from are worshipped either as gods or as forms which ancestors entered when they died. Thus it is likely that the Polynesians had the idea of kinship with animals before they advanced in their settlement beyond that area. It is possible that later, having long forgotten about the form the belief took in Melanesia, the Hawaiians developed the evolutionary schema of the *Kumulipo* in which man was descended from animals. Thereafter, explanation for lineage from animal gods, when addressed at all, was attached to evolution.

18   There are a number of other creation accounts which were well known in Hawai'i. They are not inconsistent with the basic world-view being developed, but inserting them into the main body of the text would interfere with the flow of evolutionary thought system being explicated. Some of them are presented here.

Creation Stories Commonly Told in Ancient Hawai'i

The Hawaiians had several stories about creation, and they were free to believe any one of them. One held that an ancient mother figure gave birth to the islands. The story is told, for instance, that Wakea and Papa came together and that she (Papa) gave birth to Hawai'i and Maui. Then Wakea mated with Ho'ohokulani (some versions say with Hina) and brought forth Moloka'i and Lana'i. In retaliation Papa mated with Lua and produced O'ahu. Then Wakea and and Papa returned to each other and produced Kaua'i, Ni'ihau and Kaho'olawe. (Buck, 247-8. Malo, ftnt. on 243 has Papa and Wakea producing O'ahu. The more common version names Papa and Lua, as I have here.)

The Pu-anue genealogy offers a somewhat similar story: it states that the heavens and the earth were begotten by Kumukumu-ke-kaa and her husband Paia-a-ka-lani. (Malo, p.3.)

Another famous story is that Maui fished up the island of Hawai'i. Some versions say he fished up all of the Hawaiian islands. (Fornander, *Account*, 385. Also Beckwith, *H.M.*, 227-235.) A similar story gives the credit to Kapu-he'e-ua-nui, relating that he fished up a piece of coral which he was about to toss away when a *kahuna* told him that if he would offer a pig to the gods with a certain incantation, the coral would grow into land. When he did this the coral grew into the large island of Hawai'i. Kapu was so encouraged by this success that he fished up more pieces of coral which, with similar prayers and offerings, grew into the rest of the islands of the group. (Buck, 247.)

Another creation myth (Buck, 247.) tells of a kind of spontaneous emergence:

> Now appeareth forth Hawai'i-nui-akea,
> Great-Hawai'i-in-the-open-space,
> Emerging out of utter darkness,
> An island, a land is born,
> The row of islands stretching away from Nu'umea.
> The group of islands beyond the horizon of Tahiti.

A number of writers over the years have suggested that the stories above relate the discovery of the islands, rather than their creation, and that the birth motif is symbolic or allegorical. A combination of creation and discovery is seen in the story John Young told Rev. William Ellis that in the ancient past an immense bird laid an egg on the water. The egg burst and produced the island of Hawai'i. Then a man and a woman, a hog and a dog, and a pair of fowl landed upon its eastern shores, having come in a canoe from the Society Islands, and the couple became the progenitors of the Hawaiian people. (Fornander, *Account*, 211.)

David Malo, in a single phrase within a sentence, mentions the belief that the islands were made by the hands of Wakea himself. (Malo, 3.)

And another quite different story of creation is given by Fornander (*Account*, 212):

> "Papa, the wife of Wakea, begat a calabash—*ipu*—including
> bowl and cover. Wakea threw the cover upward and it became
> the heaven. From the inside meat and seeds, Wakea made the
> sun, moon, stars, and sky; from the juice he made the rain,
> and from the bowl he made the land and sea."

Modern Corroboration Of Sentience In Nature

1 This outlook, that man "participates in" and is "of the same nature" as the surrounding cosmos, was common to most of the peoples of the ancient world, a notable exception being the Hebrews. F.M. Cornford, in *From Religion to Philosophy*, (London: Arnold Press, 1912, Chapters 2 and 3) shows how this thought framework was common from

Thales to Plato. Owen Barfield's, *Saving the Appearances: A Study in Idolatry.* (New York: Harcourt, Brace and World, 1965) is devoted to tracing the "participation" thought—framework down through Thomas Aquinas and other philosophers of the Middle Ages to Descartes. The Western world turned from the world-view of "participation" following the publication of the works of Descartes. James Hillman, in *Re-Visioning Psychology* (New York: Harper and Row, 1975, pp. 3-8) discusses how Marin Mersenne—a monk of the seventeenth century and one of the central figures of his age—focused the attention of the intellectual world on those aspects of Cartesian thought which most strongly contradicted the view of "participation." Hillman credits him with bringing about its almost total eclipse in Western thinking.

In overview, Barfield states, "This experience (of participation) so foreign to our habit, is one which we positively must acquire and apply before we can hope to understand the thought of any philosopher earlier than the scientific revolution." (Barfield, op.cit., p. 89).

2   Robert F. Sisson, "Aha! It Really Works!" *National Geographic Magazine*, (January, 1974), pp. 140-5.

3   E.I. Mukhin, "Some New Experimental Approaches to Analysis of Complex Forms of Behaviour," *Zh. Vyssh. Nervn Deyat. I.P. Pavlova.* 30 (6) 1181-1186 (1980). An abstract given in *Animal Behaviour Abstracts*, 1981, p. 178.

4   E. Seitz and U. von Wieht, "The Influx of skuas *Stercorarius ssp* into the inlands of middle Europe in late summer and autumn, 1976." *Ornithol. Beob.* 77 (1) 2-20 (1980). Abstract in *Animal Behaviour Abstracts*, 1981, p. 116.

5   Emlen's work is cited in an article by Allan C. Fisher, Jr., "Fantastic Voyagers: The Migrating Birds," in *National Geographic Magazine* (August, 1979). This is condensed in the *Reader's Digest*, (November, 1979), pp. 140-145. This citing: p. 143. Similar work has been done by W. Wiltschko, E. Gwinner, and R. Wiltschko in Germany. Their article, "The Effect of Celestial Cues on the Ontogeny of Non-visual Orientation in the Garden Warbler (*Sylvia borin*)" appers in Z. Tierspsycholo., 53 (1), 1-8 (1980). The article is summarized in *Animal Behaviour Abstracts*, 1981 #1992-Y9.

6   K.P. Able, "Mechanisms of Orientation, Navigation and Homing," a chapter in the book *Animal Migration, Orientation and Navigation*, S.A. Gauthreux, Jr., ed. New York: Academic Press, 1980, pp. 283-373. An abstract of this chapter is found in *Animal Behavior Abstracts*, 1981, p. 100, #4583-Y9.   These abilities are also discussed by Allan C. Fisher, Jr. "Fantastic Voyagers," p. 143-5.

7   Donald R. Griffin, "Prospects for a Cognitive Ethology," *Behavior and Brain Sciences*, 1:4 (Dec., 1978), pp 527-38. What is quoted is a Journal Abstract from *Psychological Abstracts*, Vol. 64. p. 780, #7230.

8 We picture the Big Bang as an instantaneous burst, happening so fast, being of such unimaginable proportions, and resulting in such incomprehensibly vast chaos, that it could not possibly have been intentionally directed and painstakingly orchestrated. This, however, is possibly due to a vantage problem caused by the limitations of our human bodies. We experience time too slowly to observe in detail many rapidly occurring events. Recently developed slow-motion photography has revealed that there is an order in the progress of fast happening occurrences. Slow motion pictures of a bullet passing through an object show that the explosive blowing-away of the material in its path happens in exactly the pattern we observe in slower occurring explosions of greater magnitude. There is greater order than seems apparent in the process of any explosion. One day physicists may be able to detail a series of interrelated events governed by physical laws and taking place in a logical cause-and-effect order. If explosions follow an ordered pattern, it is logical to assert that the Big Bang also followed a logical, ordered progression.

Explosives experts today have refined their science to such precision that they can bring down a many-storeyed building in the midst of a city without doing harm to anything around it. Explosions can be precisely planned and executed exactly as anticipated. Is it possible that the Big Bang could also have been painstakingly orchestrated and intentionally directed by beings not limited by the human restrictions of time and space and having the knowledge to use the Big Bang as the evolutionary catalyst for assuming a material atomic form?

9 This and the following example were given to me by Professor Chester Vause of the University of Hawai'i Physics department. He said citings could be found in *Elementary Modern Physics* by Weidener and Sells.

10 David Attenborough, *Life On Earth: A Natural History*. This citing is from program #1. It will be found at 056 mm. into the program. The citing format uses this correlation (#1-VHS-056).

11 Attenborough, *Life On Earth*, (#1 VHS-267)

12 Attenborough, *Life On Earth*, (#8 "Themes and Variations, VHS-440)

13 Attenborough, *Life On Earth*, (#1 VHS-190)

14 Attenborough, *Life on Earth*.

15 Attenborough, *Life on Earth*, Segment 2, "The Swarming Hordes: Insects." First 10 minutes of the program.

16 Attenborough, *Life on Earth*, Segment 2, "The Swarming Hordes: Insects." 14 minutes through 16 minutes into the program.

Akua, Mana, And Divinity

1 Kepelino, *Kepelino's Traditions,* p. 12.

2   Malo, this author's translation from the penned Hawaiian manuscripts, titled *Moolelo Hawai'i,* which were translated by Emerson as *Hawaiian Antiquities.* (Microfilm files, Hamilton Library, University of Hawai'i.) Chapter 35.

3 Kepelino, *Kepelino's Traditions,* pp. 54-5.

4 Pogue, John F. *Moolelo of Ancient Hawai'i.* 1858. Translated by Charles W. Kenn. Honolulu: Topgallant, 1978. p. 32-3 of Hawaiian text. *Ina make ke kino, hele no ka Uhane me ke ano o ke kino,* Author's translation: "When the body dies, the *'uhane* goes about in the shape of the body."

5 Beckwith, *Kumulipo,* p.91-2 (lines 581-9).

6 Pogue, *Moolelo of Ancient Hawai'i.* pp. 32-3 of the Hawaiian text.

7 Pukui, et al., *Nana I Ke Kumu,* p. 195.

8 I have assumed that life was thought to begin at conception. This is based on a passage in David Malo's *Hawaiian Antiquities,* Ch. 35, Sect. 2., where a young chief and chiefess come together to attempt to conceive a child with *mana.* The circumstances are such as to suggest that the child receives *mana* like that of the parents at conception. Life seems to begin at conception in other archipelagoes. For instance, the chant given to Richard Taylor and quoted in *Te Ika A Maui* (London, 1870) at every stage begins the evolution of things with conception.

9 For examples see: *Fornander Collection,* Vol. VI, p. 370, ftnt. 42; Mary Kawena Pukui, E.W. Haertig, and Catherine A, Lee, *Nana I Ke Kumu.* Vol. I. Honolulu: Queen Liliuokalani Children's Center, 1972, p. 194; and Nathaniel B. Emerson, *Pele and Hiiaka: A Myth from Hawai'i.* Honolulu: Honolulu Star-Bulletin, 1915, p. 81.

10 The "Lamentation for Young Ka'ahumanu" in the *Fornander Collection,* Vol. VI, pp. 451-457, mentions place after place where the bereaved "sees" his deceased beloved as he narrates his chant. She is present in each place as rapidly as he shifts his thought.

11 *Fornander Collection,* Vol. VI, p. 429. Also on p. 455, line 110.

12 Conclusions about the knowing abilities of the deceased spirit are taken from stories and newspaper articles collected by the author over the years.

13 For example, see "A Lamentation for Young Kaahumanu," *Fornander Collection,* Vol. VI, p. 454, line 96.

14 Pukui et al., *Nana I Ke Kumu,* pp. 115-118.

15 Pukui et al., *Nana I Ke Kumu*, pp. 46 and 168.

16 Pukui et al., Ibid., p. 80.

17 Pukui et al., Ibid. pp. 161-2. Also see Pogue, op.cit., p. 58. Spirit possession: Hawaiians distinguised between inspiration (*ho'oulu 'ia* or *kihei pua*) and possession (*noho*).

18 Michael Kioni Dudley, *A Philosophical Analysis of Pre-European-Contact Hawaiian Thought*, pp. 201-9.

19 William Mariner, *Tonga Islands William Mariner's Account*, 4th ed. Translated by John Martin, M.D. 1817. rpt. Tonga: Vava'u Press, 1981, p. 301. Robert Wood Williamson, *Religion and Social Organization In Central Polynesia*, Vol. I, Edited by Ralph Piddington. Cambridge: University Press, 1937, p. 14.

20 Kramer, Augustin. *Die Samoa-Inseln*. 2Bd. Stuttgart, 1901-2. A translation by Brother Henry, titled *Samoan Islands* is available in bound mimeograph form, Pacific Collection, Hamilton Library, University of Hawai'i, Manoa. This citing is taken from p. 189 of that translation. Williamson, in *Rel. and Soc. Org.* cites the German text at p. 108. See also Charles Wilkes, *Narrative of the U.S. Exploring Expedition During the Years of 1838, 1839, 1840, 1841, 1842*. Philadelphia, 1845. Volume II, p. 131.

21 Metraux, *Ethnology, op.cit.*, p. 310.

22 See Mariner, *Tonga Islands*, p. 301, and Williamson, *Rel. and Soc. Org.*, Vol. I, pp. 13-4 for Tonga. See Kramer, *Samoa Islands*, p. 189, and Williamson, ibid., pp. 10-11, for Samoa.

23 Malo, *Hawaiian Antiquities Moolelo Hawai'i*. Translated by Nathaniel B. Emerson. 1898. rpt. Honolulu: Bishop Museum Press, 1971, pp.114-5.

24 Pukui, et al., *Nana I Ke Kumu*, pp. 195-6. A description of *ho'omanamana* is given in a footnote by Emerson to David Malo's *Hawaiian Antiquities* on page 118: "The *'unihipili* then was a deity that was supposed to have been induced by incantation to take up its residence in an image, a dead body, or a bundle of bones, and that that was endowed with malignant power, *mana*, as a result of the *hoo-manamana*, prayers and sacrifices, that were offered to it. When the worship and offerings ceased, its power and subserviency to its *kahu*, caretaker and author, came to an end."

25 J.S. Emerson, "The Lesser Hawaiian Gods." A paper read before the Hawaiian Historical Society, April 7, 1892. This paper is published in *The Kahunas*, edited by Sibley Morrill. Boston: Brandon, 1968, p. 41.

26 Author's translation, taken from the microfilm of the Hawaiian manuscript, Moolelo Hawai'i, by David Malo, which was translated as *Hawaiian Antiquities*. Chapter 29.

27 The philosophical development underlying the Hawaiian practice of deification follows upon a paradigm shift made in Polynesian thought by the Hawaiians.   This footnote will show the contrast of the *ho'omanamana* genre of deification with what preceded it in other island groups.

The Tongans believed that their nobles and *matabooles* went to Bolotoo after death. There the higher ranking nobles shared all of the attributes common to the original gods, and they could return to inspire the priests and visit their relatives. (Mariner, 301; Wilkes, Vol. II, p. 132) While these deceased higher-ranking personages were called gods in Tonga, Mariner makes no mention of any kind of deification rite, even though he describes the funerals of the highest ranking Tongans in full detail. It is clear from his work, rather, that the high ranking simply assumed divinity once they were in Bolotoo, a reward of their station.

Samoans believed that their nobles went to Pulotu after death and that the commoners went to Salefe'e. Pulotu is the *nu'u o aitu*, the land of spirits, where the nobles dipped in the *vaiola*, the life-giving water, and became rejuvenated and glorified. It was known by the living that this was what they had done and thus "they were frequently honored as *tupua*, divine, and even their earthly husk when embalmed was held as sacred, as a 'sun-dried god,' *fa'aatualalaina*," (Kramer, p. 189) and was prayed to as divine. Although the bodies of these high ranking Samoans were mummified, there is no mention in Kramer, Brown, Stair, Wilkes, Henry, Williamson, or Mead of any kind of deification service for them, and when any of these writers do mention that *tupua* are deified humans, it seems clear that they are referring to the deification which takes place in the *vaiola* in Pulotu, not to anything that happens on earth.

On Easter Island the nobleman (*ariki-paka*) is thought to exercise power over nature, through his *mana* and his knowledge of rites. And his *mana* is thought to reside in his skull after death, where it can be useful in multiplying chickens. The islanders carve the skulls and place them in the stone hen houses to make the hens fertile. There are somewhat similar customs regarding skulls in the Marquesas and in New Zealand. (Metraux p. 266-7) In these cases the bones of the deceased and the *mana* within them are used to help the living, but the *mana* automatically remains in the skull after death; there is no deification rite to call it there. Metraux and Routledge both speak of "spirits of the deified dead," but neither mentions any process. It is quite likely that these deified dead are simply deified by proclamation like those of Tonga and Samoa.

There are two teachings in Tahiti. One is the belief that chiefs, members of the upper class, and Arioi Society members went to Rohutu-noanoa, a pleasant place, after death, and that everyone else went to *po*. (Williamson, Fly-page at beginning of the book, Religion and Cosmic Beliefs) A second belief is that all of the dead are treated equally, and that some are allowed to go to Paradise, Rohutu-noanoa, while others are directed to a kind of purgatory by the god Ta'aroa, from which, after about a year, they are allowed to return to the earth as inferior gods called *'oromatua.* Some of these, the *'oromatua maitatai* (good *'oromatua*), again enter into their own skulls as family gods or guardian spirits. (T. Henry, p. 202) Spirits of the dead reinhabiting their bones is very close to the concept of an *'unihipili* in Hawai'i, but outside of Hawai'i, the process for calling a spirit back into its bones seems to be unknown. Babies who had not seen the light of day, according to the Tahitians, were permitted to enter bodies of fish. (T. Henry, p.200).

Best describes a class of gods among the New Zealand Maoris, which is likely their further development of this Tahitian idea: the *atua kahu* is the spirit of a deceased for whom no funeral ceremony has been performed and who because of this inhabits the body of a some nearby animal, then growing into a powerful daemon. (Best, p. 205) Again, there is no deification here. "Bones of the dead were sometimes used in rites in former times, for they seem to possess much inherent *mana*," says Best. (Best, p. 377) This is similar to the Easter Island belief. And, like Easter Island, the *mana* of itself remained in the bones. The Hawaiian differed from his Polynesian brothers in that he himself was physically and spiritually instrumental in the creation of his gods, except for the very few which he initially brought into the islands.

Kino Lau: Assuming Multiple Forms

1 The concept of *kino lau* grew out of related ideas commonly found in Polynesia, such as the belief that spirits of the deceased for whom no funeral was performed could enter animals or other nature forms. (Cf. Mead, pp. 147 and 157; Metraux, p. 309; and T. Henry, p. 200.) But there was no exact counterpart in any other part of Polynesia to the Hawaiian systematic theory of the relations between the many animal and vegetable forms and nature gods or spirits. (Handy, "Totemism," p.54.)

2 These examples are found in the Maui section of the fifteenth *wa* of the *Kumulipo*.

3 Beckwith, *Kumulipo*, p. 114.

4 Kamakau, *Ka Po'e*, p. 86. Handy notes that *kalo*, sugar cane, bamboo, *popolo*, the *palai* fern, wild ginger, carver's adzes, owls, erect stones, spring water, rain and running fresh water, and coral in the sea are all *kino lau* of Kane. Handy, "Totemism," *passim.*

5 Handy, "Totemism," p. 44.

6 Chapter 31. Section 18-20. The Hawaiian text must be used here. Emerson, the translator, totally misreads the Hawaiian.

> O ka poe hewahewa kekahi manao ia he mea mana, ua manao ia lakou he
> poe like me ka poe kaula, a me na makaula. Ka ike i na uhane o kanaka. he
> wanana no nae lakou like me na kaula...Aka he nui ke ano o na
> hewahewa....Ina i aloha nui kekahi i kana kane, hewahewa no. Pela no ke

aloha nui ke kane i kana wahine, hewahewa no. Pela no ka poe a hau i
manao nui ma kekahi mea, hewahewa kekahi, he hewahewa ole kekahi.

   Author's translation: "People in a state of ecstasy were thought to
be people filled with *mana*. They were thought to be people of the
same nature as the prophets and seers. They knew the souls of men.
They prophecied like the prophets....Many were the kinds of
ecstasy....If one was in deep love for her man, here might be ecstasy.
Likewise, the great love of a man for his woman might rise to
ecstasy. In the same way, of the people of prayer who meditated
deeply on some thing, some reached ecstasy, some did not.

7 There is a traditional *heiau huna* or meditation *heiau* on the property
of the *kahuna* Sam Lono in Haiku Valley, Kane'ohe, O'ahu.

8 Martha Beckwith, *Hawaiian Mythology*, p. 53.

9 *"He Kanikau No Pe'ape'a,"* *Fornander Collection*, Vol VI, p. 429.

Pairing In The Universe

1 Beckwith, *Hawaiian Mythology*, p. 3.

2 These lines are taken from the first *wa* of the *Kumulipo*, Queen
Liliuokalani's translation. 1897. Boston: Lee and Shepherd. rpt. Kentfield:
Pueo Press, 1978.

3 Rubellite Kawena Johnson, *Kumulipo*, Vol. I, Honolulu: Topgallant,
1981 p. 27.

4 Johnson, *Kumulipo*, p. 29.

5 Beckwith, *Kumulipo*, p. 50

6 "The budding leaves (*mu'o*) of the *pohuehue* were also used ritually
to aid or speed childbirth when a woman had labored in vain for some
time.   With the right hand five leaves were plucked, while Ku was
invoked to come and help the woman.   The woman chewed and
swallowed these five *mu'o*. With the left hand five *mu'o* were plucked,
while Hina was invoked. These were mashed and the pulp was rubbed
on the woman's abdomen.   Quickly thereafter the child would slip
out.(Handy and Handy, Native Planters, p. 240.)
   "Either sweet-potato vines or pohuehue, both of which have a milky
white latex, were used to slap the breasts of a mother of a newborn child,
to cause her milk to flow. While slapping the right side, Ku was prayed
to; while slapping the left side, Hina.(Handy and Handy, *Native Planters*,
p. 240).

Environmental Ethics In Hawai'i

1 David Malo, *Hawaiian Antiquities Moolelo Hawai'i* trans. by Nathaniel B. Emerson. 1898. rpt. (Honolulu: Bishop Museum Press, 1971), page 156. (Author's revision of translation by Emerson.) A similar prayer is found in his chapter on the *luakini heiau:* "Ola no ke alii, a lu, a ola, ola ke aina, ia oe, Kane, ke akua ola. Let there be life to the chief, and produce and life, life to the land, through you, O Kane, the living god. (Ibid., 185.)

2 *Fornander Collection*, No. VI, p. 144.

3 *Fornander Collection*, No. VI, p. 32.

4 William Ellis, *Polynesian Researches Hawai'i* rpt. Rutland: Tuttle, 1969, pp. 212-3.

5 Samuel M. Kamakau, *The Works of the People of Old: Na Hana a ka Po'e Kahiko* trans., from the Newspaper *Ke Au 'Oko'a* by Mary Kawena Pukui, ed. by Dorothy B. Barrere, (Honolulu: Bishop Museum Press, 1976) pp. 23-38.

6 *Fornander Collection*, VI, p. 30-2.

7 E.S. Craighill Handy, *Polynesian Religion*, p. 299.

8 E.S. Craighill Handy, *Polynesian Religion*, pp. 210-11. The quotation from Handy continues: ...The gods, man-like in their nature, were present at the feasts. The dancing roused their passions, and they sought the satisfaction of their desire with their female mates (in their various other *kino lau*)....There would be many children of the nature fathers—many breadfruit, taro, bananas, potatoes, many fish—and there would be many human children, both because the procreative power seated in human fathers was released and freely spent, and because the nature fathers, from whom or through whom this power came to men, was aroused to impregnate the mothers of nature."

Handy seems to think that the dancers mimicked the gods, and the gods, seeing themselves as aroused in their mimed selves (the dancers) became aroused. But another view seem more likely. F.M. Cornford, *From Religion to Philosophy*, p. 77, presumably following upon Levy Bruhl, and talking about early man, comments that in his view that there was a continuum between himself and nature—a non-distinction between himself and the rest of nature—when he danced, his actions effected what he wanted done. "The rainmakers believe themselves simply to be 'making rain,' not to be imitating rain, so as to cause real rain to fall later," he writes. In Cornford's view, man performed effecting rain dances and so forth because he could not yet distinguish himself from nature. I disagree with the reason he gives, thinking that while early man fully distinguished himself from nature, he purposefully and mystically blended himself with nature anew. I am grateful to Cornford, however, for the insight that man is not miming nature, but rather *is* nature, when dances. This seems to be a very logical explanation for what is going on in Hawaiian thought. Only men danced the fertility dances in the *heiau*. Their sexual gestures would not have been very stimulating to their heterosexual gods. But if they were one with the gods, their actions and those of the gods would have been identical. If they were also one with nature, their actions would have effected the fertilization of nature. There are a number of hints that the dancers did indeed invite the gods to indwell them. (There is, for instance, a short prayer given in Pukui-Elbert *Dictionary* at *ulu* [which itself means "enter and inspire"]: *"E ulu, e ulu kini o ke akua, ulu o Kane me Kanaloa....*Enter and inspire, may myriads of spirits enter and inspire, including Kane and Kanaloa." See also the prayer given by Emerson in *Unwritten Literature* pp. 46-7 for the beginning of a *hula* performance: *E ola ia'u, i ka malihini; a pela hoi na kamaaina, ke kumu, na haumana, ia oe, e Laka. E Laka ia Pohaku i ka wawae. E Laka i ke kupe'e. E Laka ia Luukia i ka pa-u; e Laka i ke kuhi; e Laka i ka leo; e Laka i ka lei. E Laka i ke ku ana imua o ke anaina*) That they blended themselves with nature as they danced also seems likely. Feelings of oneness with surrounding nature are not uncommon among *hula* dancers. I have adopted this view of what is happening in the *hula*. Further, I think it is a prime instance of common men directly influencing nature in the same way that the chief nourishes nature when all is *pono*.

9 Pukui, Haertig and Lee, *Nana I Ke Kumu*, pp. 190-2.

10 Elspeth P. Sterling and Catherine C. Summers, *Sites of Oahu*, Honolulu: Bishop Museum Press, 1978, p. 118. Site 235.

11 Beckwith, *Hawaiian Mythology*, pp. 19 and 22.

12 A sign near the rock posted by the State office of Land and Natural Resources relates this. The deeds attributed to all of the stones discussed in the last three paragraphs were actually attributed to beings within the stones, who whether human or divine, would be classed as *akua* rather than matter.

13 *Fornander Collection*, VI, p. 118.

14 E.S. Craighill Handy and Mary Kawena Pukui, *The Polynesian Family System in Ka'u, Hawai'i* (Rutland: Tuttle, 1972), p. 177.

15 References for this are found *Resource Units in Hawaiian Culture* by Donald D. Kilolani Mitchell, Honolulu: Kamehameha Schools Press, 1982, p. 261, and Beckwith's *Hawaiian Mythology*, p. 17. It is a commonly heard dictum in Hawai'i today.

16 This is recorded in Donald Mitchell's *Resource Units*, p. 261.

17 Beckwith, *Hawaiian Mythology*, p. 144.

18 Handy and Handy, *Native Planters*, p. 74.

19 Handy and Pukui, *The Polynesian Family System*, p. 115.

20   Handy and Handy, *Native Planters*, p. 22.

Some other rules observed by the Hawaiians follow here:

One should not whistle after dark. To do so invites a spirit from out of the night to participate in some prank, with the whistler its victim. (Napua Stevens Poire, "Night Marcher's Scared Her," *Honolulu Advertiser*, October 31, 1971.)

A set of rules had to do with the the lightning and with the thunder which was thought to be the voice of the god Kāne-hekili (Kāne the thunderer):

"Nobody spoke in whispers, as that offended him....No
exclaiming at the thunder or lightning was allowed. Pointing with
the finger was never allowed [anyway], so whatever we saw in the
sky, whether flash or streak of lightning, we never pointed at it. A
pointed finger was always an offense to the gods. (E.S. Craighill
Handy and Elizabeth Green Handy, *Native Planters in Old Hawai'i*,
Bernice Pauahi Bishop Museum Bulletin No. 233. Honolulu: Bishop
Museum Press, 1972, pp. 32-33.)

Hala is the Hawaiian word for the "pandanus tree" and its fruit. *Hala* also means "offense or sin" and "failure." And among its meanings as a verb is "to die." One never wears a lei of *hala* fruit when going on an important venture because *hala* means failure. And dreams of the *hala* are thought to be harbingers of death. (Pukui-Elbert *Hawaiian Dictionary*, p. 48.)

Hawaiians also took special care of a baby's remnant umbilical cord (*piko*) when it dried and fell, ensuring that rats would not get at it. It was thought that if a rat ate a baby's *piko*, the child would become a thief. (Pukui, Haertig and Lee, *Nana I Ke Kumu*, pp. 183-4.)

21   Gutmanis, *Na Pule Kahiko*, p. 106. Minor revisions by author.

22   Malo, p. 177, Minor revisions by author.

23   June Gutmanis, *Na Pule Kahiko*, p. 72. Minor revisions by author both to Hawaiian text and its translation.

24   Marie C. Neal, *In Gardens of Hawai'i*, B.P. Bishop Museum Special Publication No.40. Honolulu: Bishop Museum Press, 1948, p. 625. quoted in E.S. Craighill Handy and Elizabeth Green Handy, *Native Planters in Old Hawai'i*, *Bernice Pauahi Bishop Museum Bulletin* No. 233. Honolulu: Bishop Museum Press, 1972, p. 240.

25   Gutmanis, *Na Pule Kahiko*, p. 82.

Elsewhere Gutmanis gives a prayer to stop the rain:

Malie	Calm
Malie ka ua i Poha-kea	Calm is the rain at Poha-kea
Makai he ua	Seaward is the rain
Mauka he ua	Upland is a rain

Kiola   Throw
Kiola ka ua i kou luawai.   Throw the rain into your well.
(Gutmanis, *Na Pule Kahiko*, p. 102.)

26 Aldo Leopold, *The Sand County Almanac*, p. 223 as quoted in Thomas W. Overholt and J. Baird Callicott, *Clothed-In-Fur And Other Tales: An Introduction To An Ojibwa World View* (Washington: University Press of America, 1982). p. 155.

27 Nathaniel B. Emerson, *Pele and Hiiaka A Myth from Hawai'i* (Honolulu: Honolulu Star-Bulletin Press, 1915), p. 199.

28 Mary Kawena Pukui, Samuel H. Elbert and Esther T. Mookini, *Place Names of Hawai'i*, (Honolulu: University Press of Hawai'i 1976), p. 267.

29 E.S. Craighill Handy and Elizabeth Green Handy, *Native Planters in Old Hawai'i: Their Life, Lore and Environment*. Bernice Pauahi Bishop Museum Bulletin 233, (Honolulu: Bishop Museum Press, 1972). p. 42-3.

The Special Place Of The Chief

1 See E.S. Craighill Handy, *Polynesian Religion*, Bishop Museum Bulletin. No. 34. 1927. rpt. (Millwood: Kraus, 1971), pp. 138-143; and Alfred Metreaux, *Ethnology of Easter Island* Bernice P. Bishop Museum Bulletin 160. 1940. rpt. (Honolulu: Bishop Museum Reprints, 1971), p. 133.
The presence of this idea in the earlier settled islands, Samoa and Easter Island, as well as in Tahiti, indicates that it was an early idea which was also brought into Hawai'i with the first migration.

2 Roger Keesing, in his lecture, *"Mana* Revisited," (given at the University of Hawai'i, Manoa on May 20, 1983), shed light on the meaning of '*Amama*. It occurs in Melanesia and Micronesia as a variant of the word *"mana,"* and means "Let it happen."

3 The Makahiki ceremony itself is very ancient. A number of its main activities are carryovers and adaptations of ancient rites which have no meaning in Hawai'i. It is performed at the time of the rise of the Pleides on the eastern horizon at dusk, just as it is in lands where this occasion marks the harvest time. But there is no harvest time in Hawai'i, since the main staple, *kalo*, grows year round. Likewise very little of nature can be observed "dying" for the winter in Hawai'i. Yet this rite of killing to make new birth possible continued to be practiced.

4 Malo, *Hawaiian Antiquities*, p. 148.

5 Archibald Campbell, *A Voyage Around the World, from 1806-1812*, Honolulu: University of Hawai'i Press, 1967, p. 129.

6 Malo, p. 150; Archibald Campbell, p. 129.

7 It is possible, however, that what is seen here is again the blending of the god, Lono, and all of nature in the body of a human performing the fertility rite. Such is the oneness of the king with the god and with the rest of nature, that with the symbolic death of his body, all of nature dies its autumnal death in order to be born anew in the spring. Such a reading would presume that the full meaning of this ancient act was lost over the centuries because there were no radically different seasons in Hawai'i.

8 For supportive evidence see Handy, *Polynesian Religion*, pp. 143-149.

9 Kamakau, *Ruling Chiefs*, pp. 140-141. Also, Beckwith, *H.M.*, p. 162.

10 Several versions of this story (with their references) are given an article by Lois Taylor, "The Princess and Pele," in the *Honolulu Star Bulletin*, April 5, 1984, pp. B 1-2.

11 *Fornander Collection*, VI, p. 368.

12 *Fornander Collection*, VI, p. 370. Thrum translation, author's emandations.

13 *Fornander Collection*, VI, p. 370, lines 47 and 50.

14 Kamakau, *Ruling Chiefs*, p. 222.

15 "Fallen Is the Chief," *Fornander Collection*, VI, p. 380.

The True Meaning Of The State Motto Of Hawai'i

1 This assessment is based on the author's questioning of high-school students and other associates concerning their understanding of the meaning of the motto.

2 *The Polynesian*, May 31, 1845 edition. This is quoted by Maude Jones, the librarian of the Archives of Hawai'i in an article, "The Hawaiian Coat of Arms," which discusses the many varieties of the Hawaiian coat of arms current at the time, published in the *Paradise of the Pacific*, September, 1938, pp. 19 and 38. She says that the unsigned article in *The Polynesian* was "undoubtedly written by R.C. Wyllie.

3 Gavan Daws, *Shoal of Time* (Honolulu: University Press of Hawai'i, 1968), paperback 1974, p. 108.

4 Daws, *Shoal of Time*, p. 145.

5 The text gives the author's translation of the king's words:
Auhea oukou, e na Lii a me na kanaka,
a me na makaainana mai kuu kupunakane mai,
a me na kanaka o ka aina e.

*E hoolohe mai oukou, Ke hai aku
nei au ia oukou, ua pilikia wau no
ko'u hoopilikia ia mai me ke kumu
ole, nolaila, ua haawi au i ke ea o
ka aina o kakou, i lohe oukou. Aka,
e mau ana no ko'u Alii ana maluna
o oukou, a me ko oukou pono, no
ka mea, ke lana nei no ko'u manao
e hoihoi ia mai ana no nae ke ea o ka
aina, ke hooponoia mai ka'u hana ana.*

*Hoopaaia ma Honolulu, Oahu, i keia la
25 o Feberuari, 1843.*

Ike maka, Jan D. Paalua

*Kamehameha III
Kekauluohi.*

Taken from the "Foreign Office and Executive Broadside" for February 11, 1843, found at the State Archives, Honolulu, Hawai'i.

Information on the overthrow is taken from Gavan Daws, *Shoal of Time*, pp. 112-5.

6 If the drawing is seen to depict the Mangaian version of cosmic origins, Breath or Life is placed at the beginning of things—in the bottom of the taproot, as first development above "The root of all existence."

The Maori chant mentioned in this paragraph is taken from Richard Taylor, *Te Ika a Maui*. (London, 1870), pp. 109-11, as quoted by Paul Radin, *Primitive Man as Philosopher*, (New York: Dover, 1957), pp. 293-5. Also found in *Journal of the Polynesian Society*, XVI, p. 113.

7 On September 24, 1984, Abraham Piianaia, who is of a family recognized as direct descendants of the Kamehamehas, informed the author that his *tutu* (grandfather) once told him that the state motto was a play on words. *Ea* means "heir." *Mau* means "be returned." It should be translated, "The heir of the land has been returned, as it should be." This translation seems strongly supportive of the author's conclusions. The chief is synonymous with the life of the land in this statement.

BIBLIOGRAPHY

Able, K.P. "Mechanisms of Orientation, Navigation, and Homing." *Animal Migration, Orientation and Navigation*. Edited by S.A. Gauthreux, Jr. New York: Academic Press, 1980, pp.283-373.

Alexander, W. D. *A Brief History of the Hawaiian People*. Sections from this work are reproduced as the chapter, "Kahunas and the Hawaiian Religion" in *The Kahunas*. Edited by Sibley S. Morrill. Boston: Brandon, 1968.

Andrews, Lorrin. *A Dictionary of the Hawaiian Language*. 1865 rpt. Rutland: Tuttle, 1974.

Attenborough, David. *Life On Earth*, A thirteen week series on evolution, supervised and produced by David Attenborough, and shown on Public Television in 1983 and 1984. See particularly weeks one through three.

Barfield, Owen. *Saving the Appearances: A Study in Idolatry*. New York: Harcourt, Brace and World, 1965.

Barrere, Dorothy B. *The Kumuhonua Legends (A Study of Late 19th Century Stories of Creation and Origins)*. Pacific Anthropological Records, No.3. Honolulu: Bishop Museum Press, 1969.

Beckwith, Martha Warren. "Function and Meaning of the Kumulipo Birth Chant in Ancient Hawai'i." *Journal of American Folklore*. LXII (July-September, 1949.) 290-3.

———. *Hawaiian Mythology*. Honolulu: University of Hawai'i Press, 1970.

———. *The Kumulipo*. Honolulu: University of Hawai'i Press, 1972.

———. *Kepelino's Traditions of Hawai'i*. Translated and edited by Martha Beckwith. 1932; rpt. Millwood: Kraus, 1978.

Bellwood, Peter. *The Polynesians: Prehistory of an Island People*. London: Thames and Hudson, 1978.

Best, Elsdon. *Maori Religion and Mythology*. Dominion Museum Bulletin No. 10. Part I. 1924. rpt. Wellington: A.R. Shearer, 1976.

Brown, George. *Melanesians and Polynesians*. London: Macmillan 1910.

Buck, Sir Peter Henry (Te Rangi Hiroa) *Vikings of the Pacific*. Chicago: University of Chicago Press, 1972.

Callicott, J. Baird, and Overholt, Thomas W. *Clothed-In-Fur And Other Tales: An Introduction To An Ojibwa World View* Washington: University Press of America, 1982.

Campbell, Archibald. *A Voyage Round the World From 1806 To 1812*. 1820. rpt. Honolulu: University of Hawai'i Press, 1967.

Charlot, John. *Chanting the Universe*. Hong Kong: Emphasis International, 1983.

Cook, James. *Voyages of Discovery*. Vol. I-III. New York: E.P. Dutton, 1932.

Cornford, Francis MacDonald. *From Religion to Philosophy*. London: Arnold Press, 1912.

Corum, Ann Kondo. *Folk Wisdom From Hawai'i*. Honolulu: Bess Press 1985.

Daws, Gavan. *Shoal of Time*. Honolulu: University of Hawai'i Press, 1974.

de Freycinet, Louis Claude de Saulses. *Hawai'i in 1919*. These are Chapters 27 and 28 from *Voyage around the World Undertaken by Order of the King Performed on his Majesty's Corvettes L'Uranie and L'Physicienne in the Years 1817, 1818, 1819, and 1820*. Historical Narrative Vol. 2, Part 2: Book 4. Translated by Ella L. Wiswell. Edited by Marion Kelly. Pacific Antropological Records, No.26. Honolulu: Bishop Museum Press, 1978.

Descartes, Rene. *Discourse on Method and Meditations*. Trans. by Laurence J. Lafleur. Indianapolis: Bobbs-Merrill, 1976.

Dibble, Sheldon. *History of the Sandwich Islands*. Honolulu: Thos. G. Thrum, 1909.

Dudley, Michael Kioni. *A Philosophical Analysis of Pre-European- Contact Hawaiian Thought*. A dissertation. 1986. Available in Hamilton Library, University of Hawai'i.

————. *The Bite of Food That Destroyed a Civilization 'Ai Noa*. A Study Module for 11th and 12th Grade Students. Honolulu: Hawai'i State Department of Education, 1986.

Elbert, Samuel H. and Pukui, Mary Kawena. *Hawaiian Dictionary*. Honolulu: University, 1957.

Ellis, William. *Polynesian Researches: Hawai'i*. Vol. IV. 1842. rpt. Rutland: Tuttle, 1969.

Emerson, J.S. "The Lesser Hawaiian Gods" A paper read before the Hawaiian Historical Society, April 7, 1892. *The Kahunas*. Edited by Sibley Morrill. Boston: Brandon 1968.

————. "Some Hawaiian Beliefs Regarding Spirits." *Ninth Annual Report of the Hawaiian Historical Society*. 1902. rpt. *The Kahunas*. Edited by Sibley Morrill. Boston: Brandon 1968.

————. "Selections From A *Kahuna's* Book of Prayers." *Twenty Sixth Annual Report of the Hawaiian Historical Society for the Year 1917*. Honolulu, 1918.

————. "*Kahuna*s and *Kahuna*ism." *The Mid-Pacific*. June, 1926. pp. 502-12.

Emerson, Nathaniel B. *Unwritten Literature of Hawai'i, The Sacred Songs of the Hula*. Smithsonian Institution Bulletin 38, 1909. rpt. Rutland: Tuttle, 1965.

————. *Pele and Hiiaka   A Myth from Hawai'i*. Honolulu: Honolulu Star-Bulletin, 1915.

Emory, Kenneth. *Kapingamarangi Social and Religious Life of a Polynesian Atoll*. Bernice P. Bishop Museum Bulletin 228 Honolulu: Bishop Museum Press, 1965.

————. "Religion in Ancient Hawai'i." *75th Anniversary Lectures*. Honolulu: The Kamehameha Schools Press, 1965.

Firth, Raymond William. *The Analysis of Mana: An Empirical Approach*. Indianapolis: Bobbs Merrill, 1979.

Fisher, Allan C. Jr. "Fantastic Voyagers: The Migrating Birds" *National Geographic Magazine* (August, 1979) Condensed in *Reader's Digest*, (November, 1979), pp. 140-5.

Fornander, Abraham. *An Account of the Polynesian Race: Its Origin and Migrations*. Vols. I-III. 1878, 1880, 1885. rpt. Rutland: Tuttle, 1969.

————. *Fornander Collection of Hawaiian Antiquities and Folklore*. Edited by Thomas G. Thrum. *Memoirs of the Bernice Pauahi Bishop Museum*. Nos. IV, V, VI. 1917. rpt. Millwood: Kraus, 1974.

Frankfort, Henri and Frankfort, Mrs. H.A., and Wilson, John A., and Jacobsen, Thorkild. *Before Philosophy*. Baltimore: Penguin, 1973.

Gifford, E.W. *Tongan Society*. Bernice Pauahi Bishop Museum Bulletin. No. 61. Honolulu: Bishop Museum Press, 1929.

Gill, William Wyatt. *Myths and Songs from the South Pacific*. New York: Arno Press, 1977.

Golson, Jack., ed. *Polynesian Navigation*. A Polynesian Society Book. Wellington: A.H. and A.W. Reed, 1972.

Griffin, Donald R. "Prospects for a Cognitive Ethnology," *Behavior and Brain Sciences*, Vol. I No. 4 (December: 1978) pp. 527-38.

Gutmanis, June. *Na Pule Kahiko Ancient Hawaiian Prayers*. Honolulu: Editions Limited, 1983.

Handy, E.S. Craighill. *Polynesian Religion*. Bishop Museum Bulletin. No. 34. 1927. rpt. Millwood: Kraus, 1971.

————. "Perspectives on Polynesian Religion." *Journal of the Polynesian Society*, XLIX (1940), 309-27.

————. *The Native Culture of the Marquesas*. Bernice Pauahi Bishop Museum Bulletin No. 9. Honolulu: Bishop Museum Press, 1929.

————. "Traces of Totemism in Polynesia." *Journal of the Polynesian Society*, LXXVII (January, 1968), 43-56.

————. and Mary Kawena Pukui. *The Polynesian Family System in Ka-'u, Hawai'i*. 1958. rpt. Rutland: Tuttle, 1974.

————. and Elizabeth Green Handy. *Native Planters in Old Hawai'i: Their Life, Lore and Environment*. Bernice Pauahi Bishop Museum Bulletin 233. Honolulu: Bishop Museum Press, 1972.

Henry, Brother Fred. *Samoa: An Early History*. Revised by Tofa Pula, Nikolao I Tuiteleleapaga. American Samoa: Department of Education Press, 1980.

Henry, Teuira. *Ancient Tahiti*. Bernice P. Bishop Museum Bulletin 48. 1928. rpt. Millwood: Kraus, 1971.

Hillman, James. *Re-Visioning Psychology*. New York: Harper and Row, 1975.

Hitchcock, H.R. *An English Hawaiian Dictionary*. 1887. rpt. Rutland: Tuttle, 1968.

Ii, John Papa. *Fragments of Hawaiian History*. From articles in the newspaper, *Kuokoa*, 1866-70. Translated by Mary Kawena Pukui. Honolulu: Bishop Museum Press, 1959.

Jarves, James J. *History of the Hawaiian or Sandwich Islands*. Boston: Tappan and Bennet, 1843.

Johnson, Rubellite Kawena. *Kumulipo Hawaiian Hymn of Creation*. Vol. I Honolulu: Topgallant, 1981.

————, and Mahelona, John. *Na Inoa Hoku: A Catalogue of Hawaiian Star Names*. Honolulu: Topgallant, 1975.

————, ed. *Kukini 'Aha'ilono*. Honolulu: Topgallant, 1976.

Jones, Maude. "The Hawaiian Coat of Arms," *Paradise of the Pacific*. September, 1938. Pp. 19 and 38.

Judd, Henry P. *Hawaiian Proverbs and Riddles*. Bernice Pauahi Bishop Museum Bulletin 77. 1930. rpt. Millwood: Kraus, 1971.

Kahiolo, G.W. *He Moolelo No Kamapuaa*. Trans. Esther T. Mookini, Erin C. Neizmen, and David Tom. Honolulu: Hawaiian Studies Program, University of Hawaii, 1978.

Kalakaua, His Royal Majesty David. *The Legends and Myths of Hawai'i The Fables and Folklore of a Strange People*. 1888. rpt. Rutland: Tuttle, 1972.

Kamakau, Samuel Manaiakalani. *"Ka Hoomana Kahiko"* a series of articles in *Ka Nupepa Kuokoa*. Published in Hawai'i, 1865.

————. "Ancient Hawaiian Religions, Beliefs, and Ceremonies," *Hawaiian Annual*. 1910.

————. *Ruling Chiefs of Hawai'i*. Honolulu: The Kamehameha Schools Press, 1961.

————. *Ka Po'e Kahiko: The People of Old*. Translated by Mary Kawena Pukui. Edited by Dorothy B. Barrere. Honolulu: Bishop Museum Press, 1964.

————. *The Works of the People of Old: Na Hana a ka Po'e Kahiko*. Translated from the Newspaper *Ke Au 'Oko'a* by Mary Kawena Pukui. Edited by Dorothy B. Barrere. Honolulu: Bishop Museum Press, 1976.

Kame'eleihiwa, Lilikala. a.k.a. Dorton, Lilikala. *Land and the Promise of Capitalism: A Dilemma for the Hawaiian Chiefs of the 1848 Mahele*. A Dissertation. December, 1986. Available at Hamilton Library, University of Hawai'i at Manoa.

Kamehameha III. (Kauikeaouli). Address to the People at the time of Cession of Hawai'i to Lord George Paulet. Found in "Foreign Office and Executive Broadside" for February 11, 1843. This may be located at the State Archives, Honolulu, Hawai'i.

Kenn, Charles W. "Letters to the Editor." *Honolulu Advertiser*. Nov. 27, 1948. Editorial page, column 2.

————. (*Arii-Pea-Tama-Iti*) *Firewalking from the Inside*. Los Angeles: Franklin Thomas, 1949.

————. A letter addressed to Leilani Melville Jones is quoted in Rodman, Julius. *The Kahuna Sorcerers of Hawai'i, Past and Present*. Hicksville, N.Y.: Exposition, 1979.

Kepelino (Keauokalani, Kepelino or Zepherino). *Kepelino's Traditions of Hawai'i*. Translated and edited by Martha Beckwith. 1932. rpt. Millwood: Kraus 1978.

Kirtley, Bacil F. *A Motif-Index of Traditional Polynesian Narratives*. Honolulu: University of Hawai'i, 1971.

Kramer, Augustin F. *Samoan Islands*. A translation of *Die Samoa Iseln*. 1902. Translated by Brother Henry. In bound mimeograph form, Pacific Collection, Hamilton Library, University of Hawai'i, Manoa.

Kuykendall, Ralph S. *The Hawaiian Kingdom*. Three Volumes. Honolulu: The University Press, 1938 - 1957.

Levin, Stephenie Seto. "The Overthrow of the *Kapu* System in Hawai'i." *Journal of the Polynesian Society*, LXXVII (October, 1968), 408-28.

Liliuokalani, Queen Lydia. *An Account of the Creation of the World According to Hawaiian Tradition*. 1897. rpt. as *The Kumulipo*. Honolulu: University of Hawai'i Press, 1978.

Long, Max Freedom. *The Secret Science Behind Miracles*. Marina del Rey: DeVorss, 1948.

Luomala, Katharine. *Maui-of-a-Thousand-Tricks: His Oceanic and European Biographers*. Bernice P. Bishop Museum Bulletin 198. 1949. rpt. New York: Kraus, 1971.

————. *Voices on the Wind*. Honolulu: Bishop Museum Press, 1955.

Malo, David. *Hawaiian Antiquities Moolelo Hawai'i*. Translated by Nathaniel B. Emerson. 1898. rpt. Honolulu: Bishop Museum Press, 1971.

Mariner, William. *Tonga Islands William Mariner's Account* 4th ed. Vols. I, II. Translated by John Martin, M.D. 1817. rpt. Tonga: Vava'u Press, 1981.

McAllister, J. Gilbert. *Archaeology of Oahu*. Bernice P. Bishop Museum *Bulletin* No. 104. 1933. rpt. Millwood: Kraus, 1976.

Mead, Margaret. *Social Organization of Manu'a*. Bishop Museum Bulletin No. 76., 1930 rpt. Honolulu: Bishop Museum Press, 1969.

Metraux, Alfred. *Ethnology of Easter Island*. Bernice P. Bishop Museum Bulletin 160. 1940. rpt. Honolulu: Bishop Museum Reprints, 1971.

Milner, G.B. *Samoan Dictionary*. London: Oxford University Press, 1966.

Mitchell, Donald D. Kilolani. *Resource Units in Hawaiian Culture*. Honolulu: Kamehameha Schools Press, 1982.

Morrill, Sibley S. *The Kahunas The Black—and White—Magicians of Hawai'i*. Boston: Branden, 1968.

Mukhin, E. I. "Some New Experimental Approaches to Analysis of Complex Forms of Behaviour," *Zh. Vyssh. Nervn Deyat. I.P. Pavlova*. 30 (6) 1181-1186 (1980). An abstract given in *Animal Behaviour Abstracts*, 1981, pg. 178.

Neal, Marie C. *In Gardens of Hawai'i*. B.P. Bishop Museum Special Publication No. 40. Honolulu: Bishop Museum Press, 1948.

Oliver, Douglas L. *Ancient Tahitian Society*. Vol. I-III. Honolulu: University of Hawai'i Press, 1974.

Overholt, Thomas W. and Callicott, J. Baird. *Clothed-In-Fur And Other Tales: An Introduction To An Ojibwa World View* Washington: University Press of America, 1982.

Pogue, John F. *Moolelo of Ancient Hawai'i.* 1858. Translated by Charles W. Kenn. Honolulu: Topgallant, 1978.

Poire, Napua Stevens. "Night Marchers Scared Her." *Honolulu Advertiser.* October 31, 1971.

Pratt, George. *A Samoan Dictionary* 1862. rpt. Samoa: Malua Printing Press, 1960.

Pukui, Mary Kawena. *'Olelo No'eau Hawaiian Proverbs and Poetical Sayings. Bernice P. Bishop Museum Special Publication No. 71.* Honolulu: Bishop Museum Press, 1983.

———. and E.S. Craighill Handy. *The Polynesian Family System in Ka'u, Hawai'i.* 1958. rpt. Rutland: Tuttle, 1972.

———. and Elbert, Samuel H. *Hawaiian Dictionary.* Honolulu: University, 1971.

———, and Elbert, Samuel H., and Mookini, Esther T. *Place Names of Hawai'i.* Honolulu: University Press of Hawai'i, 1976.

———. Haertig, E.W., and Lee, Catherine A. *Nana I Ke Kumu.* Vol. I. Honolulu: Queen Liliuokalani Children's Center, 1972.

Radin, Paul. *Primitive Man As Philosopher.* New York: Dover, 1957.

Routledge, Katherine (Pease) "Mrs. Scoresby." *The Mystery of Easter Island.* London: Hazell, Watson and Viney, 1919.

Ryan, Tim. "Navigator Learned Some Difficult Tasks, Developed Others on His Own." *Honolulu Star Bulletin,* Monday, June 17, 1985, pg. A-3.

Savage, Steven. *A Dictionary of the Maori Language of Rarotonga.* Rarotonga: Government of Cook Islands Printing Office, 1962.

Seitz, E. and von Wieht, U. "The Influx of skuas *Stercorarius ssp* into the inlands of middle Europe in late summer and autumn, 1976." *Ornithol. Beob.* 77 (1) 2-20 (1980). Abstract in *Animal Behaviour Abstracts,* 1981, pg. 116.

Shirres, Michael P., O.P. "Tapu." *The Journal of the Polynesian Society,* LCI (March, 1982), 29-51.

Sisson, Robert F. "Aha! It Really Works!" *National Geographic Magazine,* (January, 1974) pp. 142-7.

Smith, S. Percy. "The Lore of the *Whare-Wananga,*" *Memoirs of the Polynesian Society,* Volume III. New Plymouth, 1913.

Snyder, Patricia Jean. *Folk Healing in Honolulu, Hawai'i.* A doctoral dissertation submitted to the Anthropolgy Department at the University of Hawai'i, May, 1979.

Stair, John B. *Old Samoa or Flotsam And Jetsam From The Pacific Ocean.* Oxford: Horace Hunt, 1897.

Steiner, Franz. *Taboo.* London: Cohen and West, 1956.

Sterling, Elspeth P. and Summers, Catherine C. *Sites of Oahu.* Honolulu: Bishop Museum Press, 1978.

Stimson, J. Frank. *Tuamotuan Religion. Bernice P. Bishop Museum Bulletin No. 103.* 1933. rpt. New York: Kraus, 1971.

————, and Marshall, D.S. *A Dictionary of Some Tuamotuan Dialects of the Polynesian Language.* The Hague: M. Nijhoff, 1964.

Stokes, John F.G. "An Evaluation of Early Genealogies Used for Polynesian History." *The Journal of the Polynesian Society,* XXXIX (January, 1930), 1-42.

Stuebel, C. *Myths and Legends of Samoa: Tala O Le Vavau.* Translated by Brother Herman. Wellington: A.H. & A.W. Reed, 1976.

Taylor, Lois. "The Princess and Pele," *Honolulu Star Bulletin.* April 5, 1984, pp. B 1-2.

Taylor, Richard. *Te Ika a Maui or New Zealand and Its Inhabitants.* London, 1870.

Thrum, Thomas G. *Hawaiian Folk Tales, A Collection of Native Legends.* Chicago, A.C. McClurg, 1907.

Turner, George. *Nineteen Years In Polynesia.* London, 1861.

Wilkes, Charles. *Narrative of the U.S. Exploring Expedition During the Years of 1838, 1839, 1840, 1841, 1842.* Philadelphia, 1845.

Williamson, Robert Wood. *Religious and Cosmic Beliefs of Central Polynesia.* 2 Vols. Cambridge: Cambridge University Press, 1933.

————. *Religion and Social Organization in Central Polynesia.* Edited by Ralph Piddington. Cambridge: University Press, 1937.

Wyllie, Robert C. Unsigned article credited to him. *The Polynesian,* May 31, 1845 edition. Maude Jones, the librarian of the Archives of Hawai'i in an article, "The Hawaiian Coat of Arms," *Paradise of the Pacific,* September, 1938, pp. 19 and 38, states the *Polynesian* article was "undoubtedly written by R.C. Wyllie."

Glossary

aka	essence, spirit
akua	spirit, spirit consciousness; a god
akua ho'omanamana	a god deified *(ho'omanamana)* by men
akua mana	an ancient god, a spirit with mana
ali'i	a chief or chiefess
ali'i nui	highest chief; sovereign ruler of a district\island(s); the king
aloha 'aina	love for the land
'amama	Let it happen. Closes Hawaiian prayers
ao	era of light following darkness era (Po)o
'aumakua	ancestral spirit, ancestral god
'awa	drink made from 'awa root and used for relaxation and in prayer (Poly. *kava*)
ea	the living breath, life-breath, life
fafa)	Samoan leaping place for departed souls
haku mele	master of chant
hale ni'o	house for chant criticism
haole	foreigner; white man
heiau	outside temple, any place of worship
ho'omana	worship; to worship
ho'omanamana	to deify by worship, feeding, etc.
holoholo	to go for a walk, ride, or sail; to "cruise"
hula	traditional dance of Hawai'i
'ike papalua	extra-sensory perception
kahu	keeper of a spirit
kahuna	expert in an area; priest
kaka'olelo	chant critic\s
kaku'ai	deify—soul assumed into an 'aumakua
kalo	plant poi is made from; (Poly. taro)
kama'aina	child of the land; native to an area; native born; Modern:long time resident
kaona	secret or underlying meaning in speech
kapa	cloth made from tree bark (Poly. *tapa*)
kapu	set aside; reserved; sacred; taboo; law requiring reverence of chiefs or gods (Poly. *tapu* or *tabu*)
kapu system	system of religious laws
kava	plant, drink from it; (Hwn. *'awa*)
ki	ti plant; used for spiritual protection (Poly. *ti*)
kino akua	spirit body; the spirit form of a god vs. its animal or other form; one of the spirits indwelling man's higher self

153

kino lau	ability of a spirit or god to take many forms (*lau*=400); a *kinolau* of a god is one of these forms
Kuʻula stones	stone fish god
Kumulipo	a famous creation chant; genealogy of Kamehameha andKalakaua dynasties
lalo	downwind, beneath, below, the depths
lani	heaven, chief
lei	necklace
lei niho palaoa	whale's tooth necklace worn by *aliʻi*
leina	leaping place of departing souls
lepo	south, dirt
lipo	deep blue black
lewa	above, areas of sky; upwind areas
maʻi	genitals
makahiki	season, festival, rite honoring Lono, the god of agriculture; begins new year; includes games, collection of tribute
malihini	stranger, newcomer
mana	spiritual power
manaʻo	thought, mind
mele	chant or song
mele maʻi	fertility chant honoring genitals
moʻo	spirit\s that take lizard-like form
moana	ocean
ʻohana	family
palagi	Samoan word for white man; sky-buster
Pele	goddess of the volcano
po	darkness; place of origins and afterlife. See various meanings on pp. 11-12, 86
poi	Hawaiian staple food made from *kalo*
pono	state when everything is as it should be
puʻolo	bundled deified bones; *ʻunihipili;* bundle pule prayer
sentient/cognizant/ conscious	ability to think, will, desire, experience emotions, and know through extra-sensory perception spirit/soul/mind used interchangeably; the conscious human spirit which survives death
tapa	cloth made from tree bark (Hwn. *kapa*)
tapu	set aside; reserved; sacred; taboo; law requiring reverence of chiefs or gods (Hwn. *kapu*)
taro	plant poi is made from; (Hwn. *kalo*)
Te Tumu Po	an original homeland of Polynesians
ti	plant used for spiritual protection (Hwn. *ki*)
ʻuhane	soul
ʻunihipili	deified spirit; process of deification
wa	a section of a chant; a period of time
walewale	the birthing slime beneath the sea from which islands are born.

Index

155

Order Form

A Hawaiian Nation I Man, Gods, and Nature
by Michael Kioni Dudley

Hard Cover	$19.95	_____
Paperback	$12.95	_____

A Call for Hawaiian Sovereignty
by Michael Kioni Dudley and Keoni Kealoha Agard

Hard Cover	$19.95	_____
Paperback	$12.95	_____

A Green Hawai'i Sourcebook for Development Alternatives
by Ira Rohter

Paperback	$19.95	_____

Subtotal	$	_____
Postage and Handling	$	1.50
Total due	$	_____

Name_____

Address_____

City_____ State____ Zip_____

Send orders directly to:

Na Kane O Ka Malo Press
92-1365 Hauone Street
Kapolei, Hawaii 96707

Telephone (808) 672-8888
e-mail: drkionidudley@hawaii.rr.com